Praise for *Instant M...*

'*Instant Motivation* is an inspiring read that will ....y .....y. Through her clear and warm writing style, Chantal Burns makes a strong and passionate case to live with a different knowledge which she explains succinctly though fantastic insights and practical examples. I can think of many people I would love to read this book, and if they do, I'm sure they too will have a light-bulb moment.'

Linda Swidenbank, Publishing Director, Time Inc (UK)

'This is a thoughtful and deceptively powerful book that will change how you approach relationships, work situations and your own motivation. Understanding state of mind bridges the gap between how we think life works and how it actually works and this is a revelation that could benefit millions.'

Stuart Taylor, CEO, Kinetic Worldwide

'What you'll learn in this book is absolutely fundamental for improving your wellbeing and performance. I've personally experienced profoundly positive changes in my own ability to lead and to bring out the best in others. If you want to excel in business, feel happier while you do it, and be more confident, read this book. Its principles are genuinely life-changing.'

Sophie Hearsey, Editor, that's life!

'A thoroughly enjoyable and insightful book that produces a powerful and motivational realisation that we are capable of changing anything.

Chantal uses her vast experience to evidence the power of the mind and how this knowledge can benefit you both in and outside of your work.

The principles explored have the potential to change current thinking and become a catalyst for life-long change.'

David Banfield, Group CEO, Methven, www.methven.net

'Chantal has distilled her observations and experience from years of coaching and mentoring, to help us deal with our own thought processes at work and in our day-to-day lives. I wish I'd read a book like this years ago when I was running my own business. It would have given me insight into why I dealt well with some situations and poorly with others.'

Khalil Ibrahimi, Managing Director, Enreach

'Chantal manages to combine her extensive business experience with her innate ability to teach. This is a book that fundamentally deals with matters of the mind, but it's written with real heart. Read it and it will almost certainly help you with your performance at work, whatever your field. More than that, it will allow you to connect with you – the real you, the best you. Playing from that position you have the potential to be more successful in every aspect of your life. And be much, much happier.'

Karl Marsden, Managing Director, Shortlist Media Ltd

'This book delivers what it promises and so much more. *Instant Motivation* is clear, concise and easy to read. It offers you the potential to break out of thinking that limits you. It offers the opportunity to live a life of unlimited possibilities in your work life, personal life, in fact whatever life you choose to live.

Chantal brilliantly illustrates the core operating principles behind our performance, with examples and anecdotes to help you understand their scope and application.

As a healthcare professional, understanding these principles has the power to transform your practice when guiding patients to achieve and maintain their desired state of health and wellbeing.'

Nicole Rothband, Specialist Paediatric Dietitian, NHS Trust, Nicolerothband.com @NicoleDietitian

'Chantal Burns has managed to bring simplicity and clarity to a subject that has the potential to be complex.

Using practical examples and case studies, the real power of this book goes well beyond motivation and lies in Chantal's articulation of how thought works, which when embraced has the potential to have a fundamental impact on your life at work and home. A great read.'

Tom Probert, Head of Marketing, Dyno Services

'What Chantal shares in this book will change the way you live your past, your present and your future *forever*. In a complex world, the immense power of understanding that every aspect of how you experience your life is under your control and governed by your own thinking, was for me an incredible life-changing realisation. It continues to impact every aspect of who I am, how I live and my personal and business successes today. If you do one thing this week, read this book.'

Sarah Messer, Nielsen Media Director (Middle East and North Africa)

'This book opened my mind to the reality and power of thought. Provides intriguing and helpful insight into how your thinking can control or release you.'

Damon Jevons, IT Programme Manager, Aon

'This book provides a pivotal moment in our understanding of ourselves, our work and our relationships. If we are to discover the answer to the problems that face business, the economy and even the world then we need insightful leaders enabling high performing organisations.

Chantal Burns takes you on a journey to dispel the myths of motivation and success and explains it in a way that can lead to the kind of wealth and success that I believe is crucial to us all, if we are to contribute to a climate of economic and social change. Read this book, grasp the insights and then spread the word.'

Vicki Wusche, business owner, mentor and author, Telegraph
'Top 25 most influential people in property 2013'

'Understanding the nature of thought allows you to realise your truest potential. You no longer need to rely on external sources of motivation as you understand the answer is already within you. Chantal guides you to this realisation in a clear, practical and inspiring way.'

Marcela Tarazona, PhD, climate change consultant

'The title of this book does not fully reflect the possibilities available when you truly acknowledge and embrace what's on offer here. Chantal Burns creatively explains the operating principles behind performance and in doing so, reveals the infinite potential we have as human beings.

This book overturns many common beliefs, so be prepared to be open-minded. What could initially seem complex is really very simple and can be enjoyed at your leisure. Chantal's use of real-life examples throughout the book are inspiring and practical. She points us in the right direction of what should ordinarily be obvious and creates an opportunity to become completely and utterly empowered.

Anyone can benefit from this book. This teaching continues to assist my own personal and professional journey.'

Emma M., consultant social worker

'This book rocks! At last a book that gives me the elixir to a happy and fulfilling life. To know that your thinking is really the only thing that stops you from being the best you can be is very empowering. Chantal's turn of phrase is simple and so powerful, mixing practical application and examples with carefully researched stats. Bring a spare mind because yours is about to be blown away!'

Geoff Sewell, international recording artist and global CEO,
Incognito Artists Ltd, www.incognitoartists.com

'Until now I'd never read a book in a single sitting. *Instant Motivation* had me from page 4. Sometimes the most powerful, surprising and impactful truths pass us by because we're expecting something complex and difficult.

This book, in the simplest and most engaging way, delivers a message which exposes the power of thought and the relative ease in which we can benefit from it. Chantal has successfully brought together a world of great thinking with her own stunning insight, to produce a brilliantly presented and compelling read that delivers value on every page.'

Jonathan Lines, founder and CEO, The TailWaggers, www.thetailwaggers.co.uk

PEARSON

At Pearson, we believe in learning – all kinds of learning for all kinds of people. Whether it's at home, in the classroom or in the workplace, learning is the key to improving our life chances.

That's why we're working with leading authors to bring you the latest thinking and best practices, so you can get better at the things that are important to you. You can learn on the page or on the move, and with content that's always crafted to help you understand quickly and apply what you've learned.

If you want to upgrade your personal skills or accelerate your career, become a more effective leader or more powerful communicator, discover new opportunities or simply find more inspiration, we can help you make progress in your work and life.

Pearson is the world's leading learning company. Our portfolio includes the Financial Times and our education business, Pearson International.

Every day our work helps learning flourish, and wherever learning flourishes, so do people.

To learn more, please visit us at www.pearson.com/uk

Instant Motivation

The surprising truth behind what really drives top performance

Chantal Burns

Harlow, England • London • New York • Boston • San Francisco • Toronto • Sydney
Auckland • Singapore • Hong Kong • Tokyo • Seoul • Taipei • New Delhi
Cape Town • São Paulo • Mexico City • Madrid • Amsterdam • Munich • Paris • Milan

PEARSON EDUCATION LIMITED
Edinburgh Gate
Harlow CM20 2JE
United Kingdom
Tel: +44 (0)1279 623623
Web: www.pearson.com/uk

First published 2015 (print and electronic)

Pearson Education is not responsible for the content of third-party internet sites.

ISBN: 978-1-292-06573-1 (print)
       978-1-292-06574-8 (PDF)
       978-1-292-06576-2 (ePub)
       978-1-292-06575-5 (eText)

British Library Cataloguing-in-Publication Data
A catalogue record for the print edition is available from the British Library

Library of Congress Cataloging-in-Publication Data
A catalog record for the print edition is available from the Library of Congress

10 9 8 7 6 5 4 3
18 17 16 15

Text design by Design Deluxe
Illustrations by Bill Piggins
Cover design by Two Associates
Cover concept: Arati Devasher, www.aratidevasher.com

Print edition typeset in 9.5/13pt Mundo Sans Std by 3
Print edition printed and bound in Great Britain by Henry Ling Limited, at the Dorset Press, Dorchester, DT1 1HD

NOTE THAT ANY PAGE CROSS REFERENCES REFER TO THE PRINT EDITION

For my family

I love you

Contents

Foreword

It is a pleasure to write a foreword to this book.

What the author Chantal Burns shares here represents a new paradigm for psychology. In a field where there exists a plethora of psychological theories and models, this paradigm offers a comprehensive explanation that accounts for *all* human experience. It is also very hopeful in that every human being has the capacity to realise the wellbeing and wisdom they were born with.

I have known Chantal for several years now and she walks her talk. She lives the understanding she presents in this book in her work and in her personal life.

Working with leaders and teams in many settings, she brings a certainty of the fact that wellbeing and wisdom resides within every human being.

In a practical and engaging way, Chantal will reveal how learning one simple truth about how the human mind works can lead to a vast array of powerful and positive changes. This book and the wisdom it contains is the key to a satisfying, successful and inspiring work life.

Thirty years ago, after being introduced to a man called Sydney Banks, I had an insight into what truly accounts for the psychological experience of all human beings. Prior to that realisation I had been working as a Clinical Psychologist in the mental health and addiction fields and was discouraged by the limited results that my clients were achieving. I knew in my heart that there was a deeper dimension of wellbeing that could be realised but I didn't know how to reach that innate resource for my clients or for myself. Like them, I attributed my various states of mind to my life circumstances – whether that was my job, my past, my colleagues or some other factor. It wasn't until I found the understanding presented here, that I realised the true source of all states of mind.

As a Clinical Psychologist I introduced this groundbreaking approach into the mental health and addictions field with extraordinary results. I saw first-hand as people in emotional pain transformed into hopeful, happy and creative human beings. They reported a clarity with which they were able to deal with all manner of circumstances that previously would have confused, frustrated or depressed them. They developed deeper connections with family and friends and stronger relationships with colleagues. They found an ease and contentment with life, which allowed them to perform well whatever demands were placed on them.

For 15 years, as Director of the Chemical Dependency Services, I led a programme for a major medical centre in the San Francisco Bay Area. Operating from this new paradigm, my own leadership style changed dramatically from using management strategies and tactics to get the most out of my team, to one where I created the emotional climate that would bring out the inner resources of each team member, allowing them to create sustainable solutions and perform at an optimal level. I watched as my team began to work together harmoniously, with high levels of engagement. Their communication became clearer and more honest, and conflicts were resolved easily. Rather than getting discouraged, we felt motivated by the challenges we faced, which spurred us on to achieve greater results with our clients.

Several years ago I was part of a training programme that brought this education into the business field. It was a programme designed for managers, team leads, and division directors, to foster a more cooperative considerate and high-performing culture. They entered the training feeling stressed, pressured and 'speedy', without much connection with their colleagues. And just a few days later, after being presented with a new understanding of the mind, they were more connected, caring, relaxed, humorous and creative. They appeared inspired and excited about their work. In fact some of them had discovered solutions to their team problems that had seemed unsolvable just a few days earlier.

So what could account for this dramatic change in such a diverse group of high-level professionals?

It's what you'll find in this book, as Chantal shares the secret to how a simple understanding of the human experience can produce the kind of results that we have observed across many areas from mental health and addictions to education and business.

Chantal's words will be encouraging and uplifting, as you discover why you don't need to change anything about your life in order to experience high levels of inspiration, motivation, wellbeing or creativity.

Mark Howard, PhD
Burlingame, California
3 September 2014

The Big Picture

Why read this book

What if the single most important factor that motivates outstanding performance was being overlooked by the majority of the working population? And what if the solution to a happy and high-performance life is far simpler than it's portrayed to be?

There are two reasons why this crucial performance factor is being overlooked. Firstly, it's invisible to most people, which means it's not on their radar and secondly, when it is visible it's largely misunderstood. And evidence of this misunderstanding is all around us.

Organisations invest significant sums on the next cutting-edge development programme only to find that people's behaviour doesn't change and when it does, the changes don't last. Many change programmes simply don't produce the required results.[1, 2]

Despite ever-increasing numbers of high-performance, personal development and motivational books and training programmes, and more workers are reported to be struggling with stress and anxiety than ever before.

At this year's World Economic Forum where the good and great come together to debate and discuss world issues, mental wellbeing was high on the agenda with a record number of sessions dedicated to this topic. According to Harvard University and the WEF, mental health illnesses may cost $16 trillion in lost output over the next 20 years[3].

Multiple ways to communicate are expanding our options, yet they also create complexity or unnecessary distraction. We're expected to achieve more with less and we want everything now. People complain of information-overload and technology has created an 'always available/always on' culture.

The opportunities and choices that life presents are almost unlimited now, yet for many, this expansion has become part of the problem. Feelings of insecurity and worry have become normal and they come with a high cost to our wellbeing and work life.

But it's not all gloomy. This is one of the most exciting and progressive times ever. We're more connected than ever before and there's a growing interest in psychology and what it means to be human. A shift in consciousness is taking place and people are asking more fundamental and important questions about what really matters. People are questioning the true definition of success and happiness.

I've spent 27 years in the world of work. For the past 15 years I've been working as a leadership coach, teacher and consultant, supporting individuals and organisations to overcome challenges, build thriving businesses and unlock the unlimited potential available.

I've worked with thousands of people at every level of seniority, across several industries, from CEOs and sales teams to project managers and social workers. Whilst, on the surface, organisations have diverse cultures, different goals to accomplish, unique problems to solve or needs to meet, it seems that fundamentally we all want the same things – to experience a sense of fulfilment, feel inspired and ultimately be happy.

Throughout my career, I've remained curious about why some people change easily, whilst others struggle and stay stuck in old mindsets and behaviours, despite saying they want to change. How do some people stay motivated and inspired in situations where others have given up?

What allows for some people to bounce back quickly from setbacks whilst others wallow for weeks? And after major breakdowns, how do some of us get right back in the saddle whilst others can't go anywhere near the horse without a major intervention?

I've spent years trying to address and make sense of these differences using various psychological models and methods. This book sets out to explain these inconsistencies.

My intention is to clear up the misunderstanding about motivation and make this missing performance factor more visible. In doing so, I'll reveal the true source of performance where we find the ultimate leverage to flourish in any endeavour.

The ultimate leverage

For many years I'd recognised that how we think is key to our success, so I made this a primary focus of my work. As a teacher and performance coach, I've always looked for the best ways to help people thrive at work. I've sought the best mentors and travelled the globe to learn the latest methods. I've trained in and worked extensively with Neuro-Linguistics and Cognitive Behavioural approaches. I became licensed to use various diagnostics such as MBTI along with a truckload of other tools and methods.

While I've achieved great results with clients over the years, I've also seen people continue to get derailed and discouraged. Despite their superb skills and capabilities, they would under-perform. So I continued to search for the answer because I felt there was something missing – some magic ingredient.

Then, in 2009, I was introduced to a new understanding of the mind. It answered many of the questions I'd had about what causes people to thrive, what stops people from making changes and what makes positive change last. It turned my previous understanding of state of mind on its head.

I travelled to the US, met pioneers of this work and saw powerful evidence of its impact in various fields from criminal justice and prevention through to major community change projects[4].

The transformation in my own perception was incredibly liberating for me, both personally and professionally. The effortless changes and powerful results my clients began to experience were testament to this new understanding. I didn't need any more convincing.

'State of mind' in the context of this book is defined as the temporary psychological state that we bring to each moment, created by how we think and feel.

I've also used other terms interchangeably throughout the book such as *mental state* or *frame of mind*.

Your understanding of how state of mind *really* works provides the ultimate foundation to succeed and thrive at work in any circumstances and with any challenges you might be facing.

What this book is and what it isn't

Instant Motivation differs from most performance and 'how-to' books because it isn't full of techniques and strategies. But this doesn't make it less practical and useful. Quite the opposite. When you go beyond technique, to a more fundamental understanding of how the mind works, it spontaneously increases your natural ability to excel without additional physical or mental effort on your part.

What I share in this book is so fundamental to every aspect of your work life and how well you function, that you could say it's *the ultimate how-to*.

When people are learning about the logic presented here, they sometimes experience frustration or confusion – both of which are a natural part of any learning process. This normally happens because we are so used to getting advice, instructions or quick fixes, so the lack of 'how-to' can be disconcerting.

When it comes to learning, we tend to get *content or information based* approaches where our ability to make changes or get results is based on how much we can digest, analyse, apply or recall. I hope to point you in a different direction as the following distinction explains.

Prescription	Explanation
Treats symptoms.	Reveals cause.
Tells you what to do / how to do it.	Shows you how something works.
Gives techniques and strategies.	Inspires insight and realisation.
Gives you advice and ideas.	Generates new understanding, inspiring your own ideas.
Requires practise or conscious application to make it useful.	Application is implicit.

Prescription: Content-based learning

Most books and guides for improving performance and motivation provide advice, techniques or strategies. For example (the fictional) *Top techniques for effective leadership* or *The six strategies to build trust and win clients.*

They tell us what to think or what to do. They work well for the person who creates them because they come from that person's own insights, so they're responsive to their particular situation at that time.

Your own insights and realisations are always tailor-made for you. And we all have an unlimited potential for insights and new ideas.

Content based learning is like studying the theory to pass your driving test. You have to read the Highway Code and remember all the signs and what they mean. You're *taking in new data from external sources* to add to what you already know.

Explanation: Insight-based learning

Instead of telling you what to do or how to do it, this book points you to the *source* of motivation and high performance. It explains something crucial about *how the human mind works* in relation to how we function. When we understand *the logic* of something, that knowledge updates our existing understanding, which automatically changes how we perceive life. It's inevitable that a new perception will change how we operate.

Insight based learning requires no analysis, memorising or application. You're not adding more information to the 'data-base'. Instead you are learning how to leverage something that already exists within you.

If you've learned to ride a bike, you'll know that you can't think your way to balance. It's not an intellectual or analytical exercise.

Balance happens naturally when you let go of trying to achieve it. If you over-think it, the bike wobbles and you tend to fall off. I learnt that truth the hard way! It's the same with sports, playing music or any type of problem solving.

Perhaps we don't have to think our way to being motivated or excelling at work. What if that's the very thing that gets in our way?

I've spent many years teaching strategies and techniques, and whilst they can be helpful in developing particular skills or capabilities, they're not the ultimate answer to living a happy and high-performance life.

There is a deeper dimension of knowledge that already exists within the consciousness of every person. It's the core foundation that allows each of us to flourish.

The insights available from this book, will pave the way for increased well-being, clarity, confidence, creativity, inspiration and resilience – all the essential qualities that allow you to thrive and excel in work and in life.

I recommend that whilst reading this book, you temporarily 'park' what you think you know – about everything. You can pick it all up again when you've finished reading! There's no inherent value to be had from drawing on what you already know intellectually. The most powerful perspectives and learning occur outside our own frame of reference, beyond what we already know. What matters is what you realise here and now – fresh and responsive to the moment.

About the research

This book is underpinned by a unique research project that I began in late 2012 and completed in 2014. My intention was to provide insight and supporting evidence for:

- The crucial role of state of mind in the workplace.

- Why state of mind is overlooked or undervalued.

- The implications of a new understanding for our performance at work (and our lives in general).

In **phase one**, I conducted in-depth face-to-face interviews with over 40 senior leaders from a variety of large organisations. Various aspects of performance were addressed including key business challenges, wellbeing, stress, performance and decision making.

In **phase two**, I ran an online self-completion questionnaire with over 600 respondents from all levels of the phase one organisations (from non-managers through to senior leaders). It contained a variety of questions and the topics mirrored the original face-to-face interviews. The responses were measured by attitudinal statements, Likert scales, multiple choice and other frequency related questions.

I share my key findings throughout the book. Look out for the research icon

 You can access further in-depth reports via my website (www.chantalburns.com) and using the contact details at the back of the book.

FIND OUT YOUR STATE OF MIND INDEX (SOMi)

Use this free online tool *before you read the book* and discover your *State of Mind Index*. It's quick and easy to do and once you've finished the book you can complete it again to find out what's changed plus how to gain more insight and continue to benefit from what you've learned.

To complete it now, go to www.chantalburns.com/ SOMi before you start on Chapter 1.

How to get the most from this book

The first part of the book is the core foundation where I lay out the key building blocks and logic behind 'state of mind'. In Part 2, I share the implications of this understanding in some key areas of performance including wellbeing, relationships, confidence, focus, getting results and decision making.

I highly recommend you read Part 1 first so the second part of the book makes sense.

To make this book as practical as possible, I've used a mix of the following:

- *Case stories: These are actual client stories. In some cases the names have been changed for anonymity but any details, quotes or client comments are verbatim.*

- *Distinctions: I use these to clarify key points. Ten years ago I began using these in my teaching and clients tell me they are helpful.*

- *Research: I'm using a mixture of my own study and other research that helps to substantiate what I'm sharing. Where you see the research icon, you'll know it's my research.*

- *My own stories: From time to time I share my own experiences in the hope that you'll relate to them in some way. All of these stories are pointing to some universal truths.*

- *Reflective questions: These will allow you to gain further insight into the nature of state of mind and its role in your performance.*

What is insight?

Insight, or realisation, is a different way of describing fresh or new thought that brings increased understanding and clarity. As human beings we're designed to have insights. It's a natural part of learning and human beings are great learners.

Many of the best inventions ideas and solutions come from spontaneous moments of clarity and insight. Whilst they can occur at any time, they seem more prone to occur when our minds are less cluttered.

Have you ever tried hard to find the answer to something puzzling and as soon as you stop trying, the answer or direction you need shows up?

Fresh thought comes naturally to us but we're also very adept at blocking it. Human beings naturally learn by making associations and connecting things. We tend to compare and contrast. It helps us make sense of the world. Our intellect is full of everything we have learnt to date so we tend to spend a lot of time exploring what we already know. But there's a downside to this.

As soon as you say 'This is just like...', you've already made a decision about what something is or isn't and this can limit the possibility of seeing something fresh and new in the moment.

One of the reasons we learn so much in our very early years of development, is because we're wide open and curious to learn and explore.

To get lasting benefit from this book, there is nothing you have to do, apart from read it. Any changes that matter will occur naturally as you engage with what I'm sharing. A little insight is all that's needed in order to get significant value.

By gaining an understanding of the inner workings of performance, you'll find that motivation, fulfilment and a high-performance mindset are not things you have to strive for. They are instantly available to you once you understand what gets in the way.

When people learn about *state of mind*, they tell me it's not just their work life that improves. They tend to experience positive and effortless changes in all areas of their lives. This no longer surprises me. When we discover something fundamental about how the mind works, it is inevitable that such knowledge will begin to impact every part of our lives, since wherever you go and whatever you are doing, your mind goes with you.

Part 1

The inner source of performance

Chapter 1

The Motivation Myth

Why performance is misunderstood

'The fact that an opinion has been widely held is no evidence whatever that it is not utterly absurd; indeed in view of the silliness of the majority of mankind, a widely spread belief is more likely to be foolish than sensible.'

Bertrand Russell

If you watch any major sporting event, you'll see outstanding athletes under-perform despite months of training. It doesn't matter how great they were last week or even yesterday. They can have a wealth of experience, highly honed skills and the right support, but does this guarantee an exemplary performance? All the evidence suggests that it doesn't and we see many examples of this in every other field too.

So if it isn't skills and experience, then what is the real decider in terms of your ability to excel? What allows you to flourish in the face of challenges and stay calm in the eye of the storm? What motivates you to do the right thing?

There's no doubt that being in a good frame of mind and feeling inspired, optimistic and engaged are essential for doing our best work. Yet when it comes to thriving at work, there is one fundamental misperception that this book aims to address. It relates to the crucial role that our thinking plays in performance and to what governs *how* we think.

I remember watching Andy Murray compete at Wimbledon in 2012. Here was a world-class player losing his form on the court. He had the skills and capability to win the match but in the moment of play what did it really come down to? You could see him getting progressively more agitated and as his agitation increased his game dropped. The following year, he came back with a new attitude and he won Wimbledon.

Outside the world of sport, when you ask people what determines their ability to do their best work, you'll get a variety of answers including self-confidence, past experience, good relationships, great working environment, strong leadership, the right skills. The options are many and varied.

Similarly, when you ask people what de-rails or de-motivates them at work, you'll hear a host of reasons such as workload, poor management, lack of time, tight deadlines or too much stress, to name a few. To most people, it seems as if there are multiple causes for their ups and downs. This widespread belief – that there are multiple causes – is part of the problem and also points to the answer.

What if there is one fundamental cause and everything else is simply a symptom of that?

There's no denying that each of us deals with a variety of challenges, sometimes on a daily basis. The great news is that there's one unifying factor that accounts for how we perceive and handle all those challenges.

Each of us moves in and out of different states of mind throughout the day, every day. It's your understanding of what's behind this that determines how well you play the game of work. It's the ace in your performance pack.

Most 'state of mind' books are focused on how to get into a better state. They tell us to change our thinking. They suggest we think more positively. What I'm sharing here is different.

What if we didn't have to change our thinking? What if it's easier than that?

My aim is to show you why understanding state of mind is the most crucial yet overlooked factor that explains the highs and lows of performance and sheds light on why some people excel while others struggle when faced with the same problems or challenges.

In the domain of sport, the importance of a person's psychological state has been recognised for several years. Many of the world's top athletes and sportspeople have performance coaches whose sole job is to help them improve their mental game as opposed to their technical skills.

Whether it's the penalty shoot-out in a football match or game point in a tennis tournament, there's one thing that matters above all else. Can they keep a clear head? Can they focus in this one precious, game-defining moment or will self-doubt and hesitation overwhelm them and take them out of the game?

Skills and knowledge are crucial – I wouldn't undergo surgery if the surgeon didn't have the know-how and qualifications to do the job. But mental clarity is always the deciding factor in our performance. The ability to develop skills and use them wisely and effectively is a function of your clarity of mind.

Whilst we see countless examples in the sports arena, the significance of clear thinking is crucial in *all* sectors, regardless of the type of work a person is doing.

Whether you're a schoolteacher, singer, doctor, engineer or sales manager – whatever your role – understanding the nature of thought is fundamental. It's the difference that makes the difference. It just so happens that in terms of performance, sport is the place where state of mind has been most respected and most visible until now.

In the past few years, psychological wellbeing has become more widely acknowledged in organisations as a significant factor in the performance and productivity of employees. As with all other high-performance qualities, mental clarity and wellbeing is a by-product of understanding how thought works.

Clients sometimes ask me whether state of mind always matters. For example, is it still important if you are doing very mundane, routine or repetitive work?

The answer is yes.

I can recall many times when I've done seemingly mundane or simple tasks and messed them up because my mind went AWOL. I've deleted important documents and emails pressed the 'send' button and then soon regretted it. I've put dirty linen in the rubbish bin instead of the washing machine! I've missed motorway junctions because my mind was distracted and busy. On a few occasions, that cost a lot of time and almost lost me a client.

Maybe you can relate to some of these. How has an anxious, busy or distracted mind got you into trouble?

In my research, I asked 'In terms of your performance at work, how important do you think your own state of mind is?'

It's evident that most people rate it very highly, as you can see in my research findings:

 81% of people think their state of mind is very important or crucial in relation to their performance at work.

From the ridiculous and funny to the serious and downright dangerous, your understanding of how thought always matters because it's behind the scenes, shaping your actions, behaviour and subsequent performance. It defines how you interact with yourself and with others, how you prioritise what's important in your life. It determines the choices you make and whether you even perceive yourself as having choices.

While most people appreciate the importance of their own mental state, when asked to choose the reasons why they don't always perform to the best of their ability at work, state of mind drops down to the bottom of the list. It gets surpassed by a host of other reasons, as shown below:

- If I'm feeling stressed, worried or anxious about something
- Lack of direction or support from managers
- Lack of control or influence
- Behaviour of colleagues or clients
- Personal circumstances outside of work
- Lack of confidence
- Lack of skills in a particular area
- Lack of time
- Workload
- **My own state of mind**

The priority of choices above makes total sense based on most people's perspective about what gets in the way of doing their best work.

What this result highlights (along with many others) is how the connection between thought and how we function and perform is not always recognised or understood. This was my inspiration for conducting my research and writing this book.

These findings are the equivalent of asking 1000 people 'How important is nutrition for a healthy body?' and 800 people saying it's crucial. Then asking 'What's the main contributor to a healthy body?' and nutrition being voted the lowest after exercise, location of home, relationships etc.

My intention is to show you why state of mind (how we think and feel) belongs at the top of the list.

So, to explore this further...

If I were to ask you what you think determines a 'great day' at work, what's the first thing that comes to mind?

Now, in contrast, if I were to ask you what you think determines a 'bad day' at work, what's the first thing that comes to mind?

Here are some findings from my research in response to these questions:

When it comes to having 'a great day at work', the top two reasons chosen are:

- If I've accomplished a positive result of some kind (78%)
- If I feel like I've made a difference (50%)

Two of the *lowest* ranked answers by a large margin are:

- My own state of mind (9%)
- If I've been in a good or positive mood (13%)

When it comes to having 'a bad day at work', the top two reasons chosen are:

- If something has gone wrong at work (67%)
- If I've had a negative encounter with a colleague or manager (66%)

The *lowest* ranked answers by a large margin are;

- How I'm thinking about things (10%)
- My own state of mind (11%)

You might be surprised by these results. It may seem strange to you that 'my own state of mind' and 'how I'm thinking about things' would be so under-rated.

The challenge we all face is that our thinking is invisible to us most of the time. We all think. We take it for granted in the same way that we take breathing for granted. If someone told you that you breathed, you might think they were slightly bonkers. It's stating the obvious, surely?

In this case, it's the elusive obvious. Thought is right there in front of our noses, shaping everything and yet it's invisible to most of us, most of the time. And that's why we see results like this.

My aim is to make the *nature of thought* more visible and give you eyes for what is always happening behind the scenes so you can benefit without any increased effort on your part.

Mark Twain summed it up when he said:

> 'Whenever you find yourself on the side of the majority, it is time to pause and reflect.'

The vast majority of people are yet to fully recognise the role of their own thinking as the fundamental driver of their performance.

So what are the implications of the above?

When we don't recognise or value the role of thought as a *causal* factor in how we operate at work, we unknowingly disempower ourselves by attributing our experience of life to something other than our own thinking.

This implies that we have little or no influence over how we think and feel. We innocently put ourselves in a passive position, often described as 'victim mode'.

I hope to show you why *how we think thought works* and not *what* we think is responsible for our good days *and* bad days.

Each one of us has infinitely more influence over how we perform (in any area of our life) than we could ever imagine.

Understanding the state of mind is the ultimate leverage for our entire experience of work and yet it's often the most overlooked and misunderstood factor.

So where does motivation fit into all of this?

Traditional definitions of motivation from Oxford Dictionaries are:

- A reason or reasons for acting or behaving in a particular way.

- Desire and willingness to do something.

There are thousands of websites, books and programmes designed to inspire and inject us with a dose of motivation or passion. Many of these are based on a common myth.

The Myth: Motivation is created or caused by outside forces.

The following distinction may help to illuminate why this isn't true and why this is good news.

Experts commonly talk about two types of motivation: extrinsic versus intrinsic motivation.

Extrinsic motivation	Intrinsic motivation
This implies that your energy, inspiration or impetus to take action or make changes, comes from external factors. Examples at work include things like incentives, rewards, pay, recognition, penalties, approval or praise.	This implies that your inspiration or impetus to take action or make changes is *internally generated* and isn't dependent on outside factors.
Extrinsic motivation is based on the carrot or stick method and there is ample evidence that this approach either doesn't work or is at best inconsistent. This book reveals why that's the case.	According to this theory, when we are intrinsically motivated, we do things for the sheer satisfaction of doing them. We create for the sake of creating and not because of any external incentives or reasons.

The domain of sales is notorious for using motivational strategies to drive better sales performance. In most sales teams, there are reward systems and various incentives designed to increase momentum and deliver results. But it doesn't always work and sometimes it has the very opposite effect and by de-motivating or driving unproductive behaviours.

For example, John and Helen are sales executives working in the same team. They are told they have to achieve a 10% increase on last month's sales target for which there's a sizeable bonus available if they are successful. John thinks 'How the hell am I going to make that? Where will I get the leads from?' He becomes instantly discouraged and deflated, while his colleague Helen is indifferent. They're both faced with the same target, the same incentive and have a similar client base, yet they have a totally different response to the bonus.

For many years I worked with media sales teams who quite often had no chance of getting a bonus because the targets were so steep and the markets were so volatile. If incentives were the reason for their efforts, you'd expect their performance to suffer when there was little prospect of hitting their targets, but it was the opposite. Every week there were always some sales people in the department who gave it their all, regardless of whether they were making bonus or not. They had a high-performance mindset. Despite dire market conditions and the absence of a bonus, they remained highly optimistic and energised. They played full-out every month.

The reason we find these differences in behaviour is because motivation is inherently an inside job. If you give 100 sales people the same target, goal or incentive, they may well respond differently to it because they are all operating from their own outlook and perspectives.

Distinction: Motivation as a state of mind vs Motivation as a strategy

Motivation as a state of mind (intrinsic)	Motivation as a strategy (extrinsic)
A natural, unconditional state of mind that generates a particular action or behaviour.	Using external tactics such as incentives, rewards or praise that are designed to make us respond in a particular way.

As babies and young children, our intrinsic motivation is highly visible. We are naturally curious, playful and motivated to explore, learn and discover new things. We don't require incentives or approval to do that. This is something we learn. It becomes part of our conditioning.

In his book *Drive*, Daniel Pink says: 'An incentive designed to clarify thinking and sharpen creativity ended up clouding thinking and dulling creativity. Why? Rewards, by their very nature, narrow our focus.' In his Ted talk he says: 'There's a mismatch between what science knows and what business does.'[1]

The nature of motivation

State of mind and motivation are often talked about as if they are two separate things, yet they are intrinsically linked.

At its essence, motivation (the impetus or desire to take action) is a feeling that shows up in a variety of states of mind such as inspiration, happiness, anger, frustration or curiosity – all of which will direct our behaviours in some way.

For example, if you're feeling angry, you might be motivated to shout, walk out of a room or punch someone. Or you might be motivated to run away and hide. In that frame of mind, your behaviour may well make sense to you. When your mind clears, and you see things with more clarity and perspective, this behaviour may no longer make sense and you might be motivated to make amends, have a conversation or take some other action.

At some level, we are always in a state of motivation. While you are a conscious, thinking being, you will be moved to think, feel and respond in a particular way.

Motivation is the desire, will or energy to engage in life in a particular way. It isn't dependent on anything outside of you. It's instant, spontaneous and always a function of how you think.

Whether you want to feel more inspired, manage your team more effectively, be more influential, improve your golf game or feel more confident - whatever change you're looking to make, understanding state of mind, is by far your greatest leverage but it's often the very last place we look.

In the next chapter, we'll explore the major misperception that stops us from being at our best. I'll reveal how state of mind really works and what this means for your motivation and performance.

In essence

- The biggest misperception about performance is the belief that there are multiple causes for why we flourish and falter.

- How we think thought works is the primary cause. Everything else is a symptom of that.

- We all have access to a pre-existing, natural and unlimited source of motivation and inspiration.

- Motivation is an inside job. It's always a function of your own thinking in any given moment.

- Thought is the most influential yet the most overlooked and misunderstood performance factor.

- Understanding state of mind is the greatest influence on how we experience work and how well we perform.

Chapter 2

How Thought and Motivation Works

Why traditional thinking is outdated

*'Thought creates the world,
then says "I didn't do it".'*

David Bohm

Imagine you go to see a famous illusionist like David Copperfield. During his show, you watch him get strapped down and locked into a large glass case. The scantily dressed assistant (because there's always one) fills the case with water. They announce to the audience that this is *very* dangerous, and there are medical staff on standby in case of an emergency. The sense of anticipation in the room is palpable.

A few seconds later, after an explosive noise, the illusionist disappears. There is no sign of him. Surely it's impossible. He was right there. You could see him as clear as day.

Suddenly he reappears from the back of the auditorium, dry as a bone, to rapturous applause. When he arrives back on the stage, he says he'll let you into the biggest secret of his career. He will show you how the illusion works. It's unprecedented. You can feel the excitement in the auditorium.

He takes you behind the scenes and reveals exactly how he was able to make himself disappear. He explains how it works and why it looks so real and true.

Then he performs the illusion again but this time you watch it from a different vantage point. Now you know it's an illusion. You understand how it works. Whilst you enjoy the spectacle, you can't be fooled by it. As he disappears, your heart once again misses a beat but then a moment later you remember how it's done.

The human experience is like this. Just as great magic tricks fool us, we're also experiencing a 'trick' of the mind. My intention is to pull back the curtain and show you what's going on behind the scenes.

We each have our own theories or ideas about how our own minds work. These differing ideas are the problem and the solution.

Your understanding is shaping everything you think, feel and do. It forms the very foundation or performance platform from which you function and it has some important implications for how you experience your work and personal life.

For example, imagine you have a meeting with a prospective client. If you walk in feeling clear-headed and confident, this will affect how you interact with them. Your thinking will shape your perspective and determine how you behave. On the other hand, if you go into that meeting feeling insecure and anxious, it will also influence how you behave but not necessarily in the best way. It's our understanding of how this works which is either helping us to do our best work or getting in our way.

What's behind the curtain?

Most people would agree that their state of mind fluctuates throughout the day. We've all had times when we feel inspired and motivated. We're firing on all cylinders. At other times, we feel flat or fed-up and it seems as if our motivation has disappeared. We can all go from feeling calm and confident to tense and anxious in a matter of moments.

So the question is, what causes these fluctuations?

What do you think accounts for the ups and downs of your own state of mind?

What takes you from feeling motivated and confident to deflated, insecure or anxious?

 When asked 'What *most* influences your state of mind?' the reasons given were as follows;

- My sense of accomplishment
- My relationship with others
- How things are going for me at work
- My own thinking/mindset
- How others treat me
- How things are going in my personal/home life
- Whether things go to plan or not
- Other people's moods or behaviour
- My finances
- My journey into work

As you can see, most people have a host of reasons from weather to work-load. As one of the leaders in my research said:

> *'It can be everything, can't it* – from the fact that the train was delayed and you had a really important meeting to get to in the morning and you had to be there at eight o'clock but the train was delayed so you're late and your whole day spirals out of control because of it; or you get into a really good mood and then your colleague comes over and she starts moaning about her boyfriend, or something...'

The biggest problem (and perhaps the only problem) that we're up against as human beings is the gap between how *we think* life works and how it *really* works.

From a very young age, most of us are innocently conditioned to think that our happiness, wellbeing, stress or success come from outside of us. Every day, we are bombarded with messages that serve to reinforce this idea.

We're constantly being told that our fulfilment, peace of mind or satis-faction comes from money, material possessions, accomplishments, job status or the weather. And many of us have discovered through our own experience that this isn't the case. For example, we all know someone who, according to their material wealth and opulent lifestyle, *should* be happy but they're not. And we also hear of people who, based on their difficult or traumatic upbringing should be 'messed up', yet they are thriv-ing.

What if your state of mind (how you think and feel) isn't determined by anything outside of you and has nothing to do with your work-load, finances, colleagues, your past or your future?

If this were true, what would it mean for you in terms of your experience of work and how you operate? What could this make available for you and those around you?

As an example, how does a relationship issue at work seem impossible on

Monday and, without the issue changing, it seems totally manageable on Tuesday.

I think my partner's humour is hilarious on some days, yet on other days the same sense of humour gives me serious cause to question our relationship.

If a demanding boss was the cause of his assistant feeling overwhelmed, then surely that demanding boss would always cause her to feel overwhelmed. It would also mean that in order for her to feel less overwhelmed, her boss would have to change. But it seems that how we feel can plummet or improve without any changes to the external conditions of our lives.

Just like the greatest illusions, things are not always what they seem.

The truth isn't *out there*

There was a time when we believed the earth was at the centre of the solar system. This was thought to be fact. Yet through the insights of Copernicus, Galileo and Sir Isaac Newton, the truth was revealed, and we now know the earth orbits the sun.

For thousands of years, bloodletting was the prevailing cure for a multitude of diseases and ailments. And in the 1900s a lobotomy was deemed the best remedy for severe mental illness as well as chronic physical pain. This seems utterly barbaric now.

There are many significant examples throughout history where our understanding of how things work has been turned on its head.

In various fields, our fundamental beliefs and assumptions about what is real and true continue to be challenged and changed. We continue to realise how little we know and how much there is yet to learn.

As we discover new truths about life, we also experience the implications of our new-found understanding. For example, when people thought they lived on a flat earth, this had implications in terms of how they went about their lives. There would have been certain limitations in terms of travel. If the world were flat, there must be an edge over which you could fall.

When people realised this was untrue, they were suddenly presented with a whole new world. Instantly, those limitations disappeared and new possibilities were born. Those possibilities had *always existed* but were concealed by the prevailing understanding.

In the same way that we've uncovered truths about the outer physical world, a new truth about our inner psychological world has also been uncovered. It flies in the face of traditional thinking and defies conventional wisdom.

It reveals that how we think and feel is independent of anything that's going on around us or to us. There's only one way our experience can work and it's the same for every human being on the planet.

Three universal principles govern *all* human psychological functioning – i.e. all thinking, feeling and consequently all behaviour.

Before I share how these principles were uncovered and what they mean, I want to define what I mean by a principle in the context of this book, to create a common understanding.

The term 'principle' is often used to describe people's personal standards, beliefs, ideals or points of view. I want to offer a different definition for the purpose of this book.

In the dictionary a 'principle' is defined as:

- the source or basis of something;
- the fundamental nature of how something works.

We could also use the words law, force or foundation as they all point to the same thing.

Every major area of science is based on certain laws or operating principles.

Principles are what differentiate truth or fact from a personal philosophy, theory or set of ideas.

A principle has the following three qualities:

1. **It's a constant** – it's unchanging and always true, without exception (*think gravity*).

2. **It explains** – it makes sense of how something works (*think physics*)

3. **It has a predictable nature** – for example, if you drop a cup from a certain height, it will always fall towards the ground every time. This is inevitable.

Flight is a great illustration of the importance of principles.

For centuries people tried different ways to fly, sometimes with disastrous outcomes. They fabricated wings from various materials and strapped them to their arms but despite using all the passion and ingenuity available, they couldn't stay in the air for any prolonged period of time.

From the early work of Da Vinci in the 1400s, through to the first modern flight by the Wright Brothers in the 1900s, aviation only became possible once the core principles of aerodynamics were uncovered. Weight (gravity), lift, thrust and drag are the four principles that explain how flight works.

Once these facts of flight were exposed, engineers and designers were able to use their understanding to create all different types of aircraft. In order to be successful they had to build their machines *in accordance* with these fundamental laws. If they violated them in any way, they'd get into big trouble – as many early visionaries discovered whilst they were still experimenting with flight.

Psychology is the science of the mind. It attempts to understand how and why we think and behave as we do.

Until the mid-1970s, the field of psychology had no core operating principles. What we had and still have is a growing number of different (often conflicting) psychological theories, models and schools of thought, which now reputedly exceed 600.

Rory Sutherland writes for *The Spectator* and is Vice Chairman of Ogilvy Group. In his insightful and amusing Ted talk 'Perspective is everything'[1], he says: 'What we don't have is a really good model for human psychology to put alongside models of engineering.' He talks about how engineers have a robust existing framework on which 'practically every idea could be hung'. About the field of psychology he says: 'We merely have a collection of individual random insights without an overall model.'

Indeed, what was missing from the field, was a way to explain the source of all these psychological theories and ideas.

The uncovering of scientific principles in 1973 was a massive breakthrough for psychology. It provides that over-arching model – a way of explaining and understanding human behaviour. And since our behaviour – i.e. our performance at work – is a function of how we think (*our psychology*), these principles have profound implications for how we work and live.

The human operating principles shared in this book provide the missing piece of the performance puzzle.

So now I want to share a brief story of how these principles were first uncovered, what they are and why they are so crucial.

Syd's story

In 1973, a Scotsman named Sydney Banks was living in Canada, working as a welder. After attending a seminar, he had a profound moment of realisation about the human condition which instigated a paradigm shift in the fields of psychology and mental health.

> **'Thought is the missing link that literally everybody is looking for.'**
>
> SYDNEY BANKS

Sydney Banks experienced a deep transformation from being a man that his close friends had observed as being insecure and unhappy to becoming content, loving, caring and wise, without any change to the outward conditions of his life.

One year later and after 14 years at the mill, he left his job. One month later, he was in Salt Spring Island, Vancouver, talking to people who had travelled from all over the world to hear him speak. Sydney Banks became a teacher of the universal principles that he'd uncovered. For the next 30 years, until he died in 2009, he mentored many leading psychologists and mental health professionals. In addition, he spoke to thousands of people including doctors, industry leaders and MIT graduates.

Whilst Sydney Banks himself had no formal academic education to speak of, he became an advisor and guide to some of the most esteemed academics. This includes being a consultant to the Medical School and the Dean at West Virginia University.

There have been several doctoral dissertations, journal papers and articles published over the years, that evidence the incredible impact of a 'principle based' approach in a multitude of sectors[2].

From inmates and police officers to teachers and school children and from social workers and psychologists to parents and business leaders, the understanding shared in this book is making a positive and profound difference to people's lives.

Why are these principles so important?

Every aspect of how you experience your (work) life can be traced back to three human operating principles. Together, they provide a logic for how we function psychologically and this applies to every person on the planet, without exception. Just as the principles of aerodynamics provide a logic for how flight works without exception.

All thought, feeling, perception and behaviour are generated via these three universal principles which are: *Mind*, *Thought* and *Consciousness*.

They are quite literally the building blocks of the human experience just as gravity is a fundamental building block of physics.

Together, they explain wellbeing, self-esteem, compassion, confidence, happiness, creativity, common sense and resilience – in fact all the qualities of a high-performance mindset.

> 'Mind, Consciousness and Thought are the three principles that enable us to acknowledge and respond to existence.'[3]
> **SYDNEY BANKS**

We cannot *see* gravity and in the same way, we cannot see these principles but, like gravity, we experience the results of them in every moment of our lives in the form of our thoughts, feelings and perceptions.

Since these principles are formless facts, they're not easily put into words so I will do my best to describe them. In the film *Enter the Dragon*, during a combat lesson, Bruce Lee says to his student: 'It's like a finger pointing away to the moon. Don't concentrate on the finger or you will miss all that heavenly glory.' In a similar way, I ask that you look to where I attempt to point, rather than focusing on the words themselves, as they could never fully describe the depth and potential of these principles.

The Principle of Mind

(Other names include Impersonal Mind, Absolute Mind, Big Mind.)

Normally when the word *mind* is used, it refers to the personal mind.

As a principle, Mind points to the universal energy behind our individual minds – and behind life. It's what makes a human experience possible.

For centuries this energy has been described in many ways by different cultures and disciplines. Scientists call it energy or intelligence. Physicists have called it the quantum field. Spiritualists call it source or life force. The Chinese call it chi. There are probably countless names used, but all labels or descriptions point to the same impersonal energy behind life.

> 'Some believe the brain and the mind are the same.
> But there has to be a power behind the brain to make it function.
> The brain and mind are two entirely different things.
> The brain is biological.
> The mind is spiritual.
> The brain acts like a computer:
> Whatever you put into it is all you get out. This is logic.'[4]
>
> SYDNEY BANKS

Whilst we can't see this energy of Mind directly (because it has no form in and of itself), it's the very fabric of all that exists – all of nature.

We're made of this energy.

The fact that you're alive, that blood is flowing through your veins and your heart is beating is because of this energy. You don't have to tell your heart to beat or make yourself breathe. It all happens naturally while you are awake *and* while you sleep.

Every day, we experience the pure intelligence, wisdom and mystery of this energy through the magnificence of nature. We see nature's ecosystems with their inherent ability to self-correct and self-regulate.

And just as earth's ecosystems are naturally self-correcting, so are we. The body's immune system is an incredible expression of this intelligence and wisdom with its innate ability to restore, respond and re-calibrate.

When my friends are cycling at very high altitudes, their blood will change to accommodate a new environment. This happens naturally, without their input. It's quite incredible when you think about it.

If I cut my finger by accident (as I sometimes do when I'm chopping and cooking), the process of healing will begin. As long as I don't interfere with this natural process, the wound will soon heal. *Resilience is quite literally the nature of nature.*

And it's not just the body that has this innate intelligence. So does the mind. We are each connected to and part of an unlimited source of pure intelligence, wisdom and potential.

A deeper dimension of Intelligence

As babies we're able to master some of the most complex feats, often with relative ease. Our mastery of speech and language are examples of this intelligence.

The notion of innate wisdom is not new. Socrates, Plato and Aristotle all taught that knowledge is inborn. Plato spoke of knowledge as the process of *remembering that which is already present at birth*. The word education comes from the Latin educar meaning *to draw out from within*.

The Principle of Mind points to this innate wisdom or knowledge as a *pre-existing intelligence*. Our individual personal intelligence (or personal mind) is an expression of this unlimited potential unfolding through us.

Each time you have an 'out of the blue' idea, a spark of divine inspiration, an intuition or a moment of clarity, you are experiencing the intelligence of Mind expressing itself through you.

In those moments when you feel deeply connected to life and part of something bigger than you, this too is an expression of this universal energy. Our intelligence as human beings is far greater than our personal minds could ever comprehend.

> 'An important thing to realise is that Universal Mind and personal mind are not two minds thinking differently, but two ways of using the same mind.
>
> The Universal Mind, or the impersonal Mind, is constant and unchangeable.
>
> The personal mind is in a perpetual state of change.'[5]
>
> SYDNEY BANKS

The Principle of Thought

Thought uses the energy of Mind to create our moment-to-moment experience of life. It's the ultimate creative tool that we use from birth until death.

When people talk about thought, they typically mean *the content* – i.e. *what we are thinking* from moment to moment. This includes our ideas, preferences, opinions, judgements, beliefs, reasons – all of which are descriptions of how we use the principle of Thought.

The principle of Thought is *all mental activity*. It includes every element of our psychological experience whilst awake and asleep. Anything we can create in our minds is Thought. All the images we see, the sounds we hear, all tastes and smells and every emotion that we experience. All of these are an expression of Thought taking form.

For example, notice what happens when you imagine eating one of your favourite foods. The mere sight or smell of good food will increase saliva, hence the expression 'makes my mouth water'. Or someone with a fear of insects starts to think about a spider and their palms begin to sweat and their pulse begins to race.

For as long as we each live, the power of Thought will flow through us.

Thought is the pure, impersonal potential that allows you to create any thought content and to experience that content as your subjective or personal reality.

> 'There is nothing in your experience that isn't first in your thinking and there is nothing in your thinking that isn't in your experience'.[7]

DR GEORGE PRANSKY

The following distinction may be helpful to illustrate the characteristics of Thought from two different vantage points.

Distinction: The principle of Thought vs The content of Thought

The principle of Thought	The content of Thought
The power to think.	What we are thinking about.
Formless energy.	The creation or forms of Thought.
Constant and unchanging.	Naturally changing.
Impersonal, universal, neutral.	Personal, individualised.
Whole, undivided. Pure potential to create any thought content.	An infinite number of individual thoughts flow through us.
	Variety of thought content that we describe as: ideas, concepts, opinions, beliefs, judgements, reasons, justifications.

The Principle of Consciousness

'Consciousness allows the recognition of form, form being the expression of Thought'[8]

SYDNEY BANKS

Consciousness is pure awareness and understanding. It allows you to directly experience whatever you think in any given moment. It also allows you to be an observer of yourself as the thinker.

The thoughts that shape your behaviour are brought to life via Consciousness. Whatever you think, you will instantly experience through your sensory system.

Thought without Consciousness is like an old-fashioned movie projector without the light. You'd have no way of being aware of the movie or experiencing it.

Consciousness is the best special effects department of the human operating system because it makes thought look, sound and feel real.

A powerful example of how Thought and Consciousness work together is during the rescue of people trapped in a burning building.

Those who have experienced this will often describe how they didn't feel any pain while they were focused on the rescue. It's not until they are outside and medical staff take over that they suddenly become conscious of their skin and the pain kicks in.

Your focus and where you place your attention in any moment, is what you will be aware of at any given moment. This is the role of Consciousness at work.

Thought and Consciousness allow you to make pictures in your mind's eye and to hear the voice of someone you care about as you remember them. They allow you to feel that rush of excitement or joy as you fantasise about a special event in the future.

At this point you might be thinking, well this is all very interesting, but what has this got to do with motivation and performance?

The answer is *everything*.

Performance is always an inside job because the origin of every action or behaviour is Thought. If we want to influence performance, the most leveraged place to start is where it begins.

In *The Relationship Handbook*, Dr George Pransky says:

> **'Change is a domino effect: a thought generates a feeling that in turn motivates a behaviour.'**[9]

We're all using the same power of Mind, Thought and Consciousness, yet we all use it quite uniquely and personally. We each have habits of thinking and acquired knowledge. Some call it conditioning. Whilst our individual thoughts are always in flux, the ultimate source of all psychological experience is constant and unchanging.

This means that our differences as human beings are quite superficial. At our essence we're all fundamentally the same. We are all thinkers who think our way through life. We are all able to be aware of ourselves as thinkers. We all have access to the same unlimited wisdom that Mind contains. We're all made of the same stuff. Any differences between us are simply a reflection of how we individually use this intelligent system that we've been gifted.

Why perception *is* reality

I worked in sales for many years. The ability to create and maintain trusting relationships is key to success in this field. One of my first managers used to tell the team: 'Be mindful of how you are coming across because perception is reality.'

At the time it sounded like good advice. Little did I know the truth that it contained.

Many of the greatest thinkers of our time have pointed to the fact that we don't experience the world directly. Aristotle, cited as the first genuine scientist in history, taught us that all concepts and knowledge are based on pure perception. Einstein famously said: 'Reality is merely an illusion, albeit a very persistent one.'

One thing on which most people would agree is that there's a world out there that seems separate to us. There are people and buildings. You can feel the warmth of the sun on your skin, see trees swaying in the breeze or hear the voices of people around you. It seems undeniable that *out there*, independent and separate from you, is a physical world that is real, tangible and definite.

Whilst this is true, like any great illusion, all is not quite what it seems.

In any given moment, your unique experience of reality is being generated via the principle of Thought and made to look and feel real by Consciousness via your senses.

As you read this book, your entire experience of it is pure perception. Whilst the book exists, it comes to you as neutral data in the form of light, entering your eyes, meeting your retina and triggering electro-chemical impulses. Those impulses are travelling down nerve fibres to the back of your brain and using a combination of past and acquired experience (you've learned how to recognise and name a book) your brain is rapidly piecing all the information together, generating an interpretation which says 'This looks like a book, therefore it must be a book.'

We use Thought to think about the past, which leads us to make certain assumptions and create expectations for the future –also *Thought*.

The following is a classic example of Thought and perception in action. I've shown this to many clients over the years with a variety of responses.

What can you see as you look at this image?

Do you see an old lady or a young lady?

Can you see both, just one or neither?

In reality, all that exists on this page are lines and spaces. Thought allows you to perceive what is *out there* and you create your own meaning. You fill in the gaps. Your experience of this image is generated by the principle of Thought, brought to life by Consciousness.

Colour is another fascinating example of how Thought and perception works.

I recently visited a bluebell wood where the ground was carpeted with beautiful bright blue flowers. Even though I could clearly see the intensity of a blue hue as I looked around me, in actual fact there was no blue out there.

Nothing outside of our minds has any inherent meaning in and of itself. What is *out there* is sensory data that we give meaning to by using our minds – using Thought.

It still amazes me that the experience of colour does not exist as an independent fact out there in the world, but instead is an experience that we create entirely inside our own minds. The role of the brain is to process the data *after* it's been perceived via our senses. And none of this can happen without Thought and Consciousness first doing their job.

In a conversation with psychologist and teacher Dr Christina Hall, she said to me: 'Perception is a mirror not a fact because what we actually look upon is our state of mind projected outwards.'

When we observe life, whether it's a past event, our colleagues or the environment we work in, we tend to think of our minds as cameras, capturing images of what is already out there and then responding to what we see or hear. But the truth is quite different.

Your mind is more like a projector, casting Thought onto a giant screen. Then Consciousness does its job and brings those thoughts to life to give you a three-dimensional, multi-sensory experience called Life.

And all of this powered by the intelligence of Mind. What an incredible system!

The mind as a projector

In the next chapter, we explore the most valuable piece of the human operating system and what it means for you.

In essence

- The human operating principles are neutral and formless yet they allow us to experience all form and all existence.

- You cannot have *a psychological experience* without Mind, Thought and Consciousness.

- The principle of Thought is the bridge between our inner and outer worlds.

- All behaviour is a direct reflection of our moment-to-moment thinking.

- Understanding how Thought works is your greatest leverage when it comes to fulfilling your true potential.

Chapter 3

The Logic of Emotion
Why control is not the answer

'We were designed and built to feel, and there is no thought, no state of mind, that is not also a feeling state.'

Jeanette Winterson

Meet Robert. He's got a full day ahead of him with several meetings and deadlines. Before he even arrives at work, he's feeling a bit flat. He opens his email and there's a message from his boss. It says he wants to meet with him to discuss something important at 3pm. He's asked Robert to clear his diary and make himself available. Robert's mind goes into overdrive. 'What does he want to talk about?' 'What's happened?' He starts thinking all kinds of things. His goes from feeling flat to excited in 60 seconds.

Where are Robert's feelings coming from?

His understanding of this will determine how he relates to those feelings and, in turn, how it impacts on his day. And that's the same for each of us.

We all know people who have a bad journey into work and then spend the morning in a low mood. In their mind, they are still on that motorway even though they're at their desk.

In our fast-paced and often challenging work lives, we don't want to let a passing state of mind dictate our enjoyment, behaviour and actions, yet that's often what happens. Unless we understand *the nature* of our feelings, we can innocently think we are at the mercy of them.

The Thought–feeling connection

If I were to ask you what's responsible for the variety of different feelings you experience, from happiness and confidence through to anxiety or frustration, what would your answer be?

I've asked several hundred people this question over the past two years – people from all walks of life and all levels of organisations.

In my research there was an almost unanimous response to this question.

91% of people said their emotions and how they feel at work is determined by what's going on around them.

The logic of these principles show us that *all psychological experience* is created via Mind, Consciousness and Thought – *from the inside-out*. This includes all feeling states from sadness and frustration to happiness and excitement.

All feelings are created by Thought.

Your feelings are the felt expression of the Principle of Thought taking form, moment to moment.

Thought and feeling are inseparable.

Thought and feeling are two sides of the same coin

TEST IT

Think of something 'sad' and try to have a happy feeling while you are thinking it. And now think of something that you know makes you feel good and try and have a sad feeling while you are thinking it.

Whatever you think, you will feel. Whatever you feel can only ever come from Thought in the moment. This is how the human operating system works.

Sometimes you might be aware of having strong feelings in a particular situation and yet be unaware of any specific thoughts. This makes sense as many thoughts are in the background, out of our conscious awareness.

More importantly, the content of thought isn't the issue. It's our pre-occupation with the content of our thinking that gets us into trouble and it's our understanding of how the system works that gets us out of trouble.

Thinking that our feelings can come from somewhere other than Thought in the moment is like blaming the car in front for your empty fuel tank.

As human beings, we operate through a *Thought-Feeling* system; This means the performance formula is essentially a *Thought-Feeling-Behaviour* cycle.

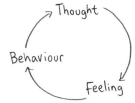

The performance formula

Here's a typical example of how this plays out day to day.

The performance cycle

A new paradigm for human performance

When core scientific principles are uncovered, they expose a new paradigm which replaces the existing understanding, making it instantly obsolete. It creates an irreversible change.

Examples in history include Louis Pasteur, known as the father of microbiology, who discovered the principles of vaccination which contributed to germ theory. After his first vaccine discovery, using the principle he uncovered, he went on to develop vaccinations for many diseases including cholera, TB and smallpox.

Lavoisier was the father of modern Chemistry. He revolutionised what had until then, been a chaotic field with many fragmented ideas. He discovered Oxygen and Hydrogen, created the first table of elements and formulated the basic law of chemistry.

William James, known as the father of modern psychology, was reported to have voiced the need for foundational principles that would explain human nature. He talked about the discovery of core principles as 'the scientific achievement, before which all past achievements would pale'[1].

James stated: 'The only thing which psychology has a right to postulate at the outset is the fact of thinking itself.'[2]

James described the field of psychology as being like physics before Galileo and chemistry before Lavoisier. About the uncovering of core principles James said 'come they some day surely will'.

Until the principles of Mind, Thought and Consciousness were uncovered by Sydney Banks in 1973, psychology was a *pre-paradigm field.*

We now have causal laws which reveal a new paradigm that explains how human experience works and, by inference, how it doesn't or cannot work.

Distinction: Inside-out vs Outside-in

Inside-out paradigm	Outside-in illusion
100% of your feelings are being generated by thought in the moment and cannot come from anything other than thought in the moment. Thought and feeling are one.	Our feelings can be generated by something other than thought in the moment. It means we have split thought and feeling.

Mixed (inside-out and outside-in)
The belief that our feelings could be coming from our thinking *and* from somewhere other than our thinking (i.e. past events, current situations, other people, future events).

Source: Based on the pioneering work of Dr Keith Blevens and Valda Monroe[3].

What does 'outside' really mean?

I'll be using *outside-in* and *inside-out* as short cuts throughout the book so it's important to have a common understanding of what these mean. It's easy to relegate 'outside' to being the material world, yet it's so much more than that.

We live in a world of external physical things – buildings, cars, people, roads and trees. There are things we can bump into and make physical contact with. But most of what we bump into is our inner world of Thought and feeling that we've innocently put outside of ourselves.

In the same way that a laser can project an image or words onto a building, we project our thoughts and feelings onto someone or something.

Like the projector analogy, our thoughts are now outside of us, part of a 'fixed reality' or a circumstance *out there*. Much of what we perceive as outside circumstances are really a reflection of our inner world of thoughts and feelings.

**We objectify our thinking – *we turn a thought into a thing*.
Anything we think has the power to make us feel a particular way
becomes part of our 'outside' because, in our minds, we have split
Thought and feeling. We have attached our feelings to something *out
there, separate from our own mind*.**

The past often becomes part of our outside circumstances because when
we think about a 'bad' experience, unless we recognise that our feelings
in the moment are coming from Thought, then this past event seems to
have some inherent power over us. But we can only experience the past
by thinking about it. And any feelings you have can only ever come from
your thinking now – in the moment.

Most people recognise that their thinking has *something* to do with how
they are feeling but most of us also point to something other than our
thinking as being the cause of how we feel at work – the boss, the traffic,
the success of the project, whether we get the result we want.

This means that most of us are living in what pioneering psychologist
Dr Keith Blevens calls 'a mixed paradigm understanding'. Hence the
term 'mixed' in the previous image, indicating where most of us are
living.

You hear this expressed when people say things like 'I need to stop thinking
about this because I'm getting worried'. But if you ask them what's making
them feel worried, they will most likely give you reasons related to the situation.
They're unlikely to say 'because of how I am thinking'.

My research highlights the confusion we all experience. As you've already
seen from what I have shared so far, sometimes 'my thinking' or 'state of
mind' is included in people's experience of work and how they perform,
and sometimes it isn't.

Living in a mixed paradigm is the equivalent of living in a world where
sometimes the earth is flat and sometimes the earth is round. But it can't
be both. It's round 100% of the time just as the sun is always there whether
we see it or not.

These universal principles show us the unbending logic behind life – that our experience can only work inside-out.

Only *your thinking* about how it works can make it seem any other way!

How does knowing this help you?

As you become conscious of the inside-out paradigm in your day-to-day life, the benefits and implications are unlimited. The more that you look in this direction, you'll have your own realisations and some of these will create small, positive changes and some may rock your world. That's the beauty of insight.

When you believe that something other than your own thinking has the power to make you feel a particular way, you will to some degree be at the mercy of that belief. It will cause you to think or behave in ways that you otherwise wouldn't.

KEY IMPLICATIONS OF BELIEVING THAT LIFE WORKS OUTSIDE-IN

(When we think that our feelings can come from something or somewhere other than Thought in the moment.)

We need to control/manage life: If the cause of our feelings is *out there*, then we'll be inclined to try and control or manage those things that we believe are causing us to feel that way – whether positive or negative.

This could include trying to change the situation or keep it the same. We might try to control or influence people. We may judge and criticise others.

We need to control/manage ourselves: If we can't control those external factors, that we believe are to blame for how we feel, then we'll try to control or manage how we respond. For example, we might avoid or ignore the situation or person involved. We might try and control or manage our emotions or our behaviour. We may blame or judge ourselves in some way.

KEY IMPLICATIONS OF SEEING LIFE FROM THE INSIDE-OUT

(When we insightfully realise that 100% of our feeling state is being created by Thought in the moment and nothing other than Thought.)

No control required: When we realise that nothing outside of us has the power to make us feel a particular way, then we don't have to manipulate or manage life in order to regain clarity or feel better.

Self-clearing system: At any moment we can realise that how we feel is not caused by anything other than Thought in the moment. This realisation will automatically remove a whole bunch of (outside-in) thinking, clearing your mind as it returns you back to the present moment.

Operating from a clear mind will always help us to see life with more wisdom and perspective. It cannot help but change how we approach things – whether it's an impending conversation, a problem or a meeting.

Let's take an example of someone who experiences high levels of anxiety when they have to speak to a large group. This is a common issue for many. It's frequently stated that people are more scared of public speaking than death. So imagine you're one of those people and your boss announces that you've got to replace him and speak at a conference tomorrow. You're told that 600 people are attending. The biggest group you've spoken to is 50 and you had a month to prepare for that.

You arrive at the venue. You watch people taking their seats. The room is huge. There's a big stage at the front. You start to feel your hands sweat. You begin to doubt you can pull this off. You've hardly had enough preparation time. People might be disappointed because they were expecting to hear your boss speak. The feelings of anxiety increase. You look at the clock and you've only got 30 minutes until you're on. The anxiety increases. At this point, you want to exit the building but they're putting your mic on. The person next to you is also a speaker. They seem relaxed as they laugh and joke with a colleague. They're obviously more prepared than you or perhaps they are used to the big crowd.

To most people it will seem like their feelings are being determined to some degree, by the situation – the room size, the audience, the lack of experience or preparation.

Whilst we might believe that our state of mind is an indication of the state of the situation, it's only ever an indication of where we think our feelings are coming from.

'The biggest human psychological problem is not that people misunderstand the power of outside circumstances. The biggest human psychological problem is that people think there is the possibility of an Outside-In paradigm.'

KEITH BLEVENS AND VALDA MONROE

As you gain more certainty about how Thought works, you'll find that you stop automatically looking outside yourself to fix how you're feeling because you realise the cause and the solution isn't *out there*.

Thought and feeling are one.
They travel together.
We're always in the feeling of Thought taking form in the moment.

The biggest challenge we face is that it doesn't look like our feelings are coming directly from our thinking. A lot of the time, it really does look and feel like it's coming from the job, the spouse, the kids, the weather, the traffic, the bank account, the holiday, the boss, the client. It also doesn't seem like the world is spinning, but it is. On that we can rely.

Thought is so brilliantly deceptive and creative which is why we benefit so greatly from understanding how it really works.

Remember that your mind is more like a projector than a camera.

Have you ever noticed that when your head is clear, and you're in a lighter feeling, things seem easier, simpler and more manageable? And in this feeling state, life seems more beautiful. People are great, funny, interesting. You appreciate the small things and you feel more at ease.

In contrast, when your head is full and cluttered, or you're in a low mood, things often seem more difficult or more complex. People are annoying, selfish or irritating. Life is less beautiful and feelings of appreciation are replaced with the uncanny ability to notice all that is wrong with your life, with others or the world.

There's only one reason for this.

Life always shows up as a direct reflection of how we are thinking from moment to moment.

But it's not what we think that matters. It's not about the content of our thoughts. It's *how we think Thought works* that motivates our behaviours and shapes our performance.

Which direction are you facing?

Which paradigm do you think is true in any given moment?

Are you seeing life from the outside-in or the inside-out?

The key to feeling motivated, happy, successful and fulfilled is to understand and recognise where your moment-to-moment experience is coming from. It's incredibly helpful to know that *we are always* responding to our own thoughts and feelings and never to the situation itself. That's the logic and wisdom of nature's design. It only works one way, whether we see it or not.

In Part 2 of this book, you'll discover how an understanding of the human operating principles is the master key to wellbeing, confidence, influence, achievement, healthy relationships, effectiveness, decision making and resilience.

In the next chapter, I reveal the truth about stress, why coping strategies aren't required and why negative feelings are your friend and not the enemy.

In essence

- Life is an inside-out experience – our feelings can only ever come from Thought in the moment. The outside-in doesn't exist.

- Thought and feeling are inseparable.

- The mind is more like a projector than a camera.

- It's *how we think Thought works* that motivates our behaviours and shapes our performance.

Chapter 4

The Truth About Stress and Pressure

Thrive under any circumstances

'The task is not so much to see what no one has yet seen; but to think what nobody has yet thought, about that which everybody sees.'

Erwin Schrodinger

In December 2013, Jonathan Trott, a leading cricketer, was big news as he left one of the most prestigious cricket competitions. *The Telegraph* newspaper described him as having a 'stress related illness' or possible depression[1]. Trott was just another in a spate of high-profile exits over the past few years. Andrew Strauss, England cricket captain, announced his retirement from the sport. The reasons reported were poor performance on the field and increased pressure both professionally and personally.

In the world of business, Antonio Horta-Osorio, ex-CEO of Lloyds and only months into the role, was signed off with extreme fatigue and stress 'due to overwork'. Early in 2014, Hector Sants, head of compliance at Barclays, quit after reportedly going on leave due to stress and exhaustion.

Important lessons can be learnt from these stories. They help to highlight the importance of mental wellbeing at work and the costs of the prevailing misunderstanding.

Headlines and statistics on the negative impact and cost of stress in the workplace are frequent. Stress is now reported to be the single biggest cause of long-term sickness in the UK.[2]

Thought is so brilliantly deceptive and creative which is why we benefit so greatly from understanding how it really works.

As you'll see from the findings I share with you in this chapter, my research provides compelling evidence for just how misunderstood stress is. Let's start with this one:

The No.1 reason people chose for why they don't always perform to the best of their ability was 'If I'm feeling stressed, anxious or worried'.

The lowest rated answer was 'My own state of mind'.

What this finding indicates is that the link between Thought and feelings of stress is vastly unrecognised. While science and psychology has moved on, attitudes and approaches have stayed locked in an old paradigm.

Traditional approaches are focused on *managing stress* and most of the books, websites and literature have a similar premise. We have a multi-million pound 'stress management' industry that offers coping strategies and different ways to deal with our stressful lives.

The widespread belief that stress is 'just a fact of life' is based on an outdated understanding. What if stress doesn't have to be managed? What if it's easier than that? I suggest that the solution to stress and anxiety is simply to understand it for what it really is.

We all have the ability to thrive in *any* state of mind. We all have the potential to experience supreme levels of psychological wellbeing in any situation. This would help us make better decisions, feel more connected to others, feel a deeper sense of satisfaction from our work and get better outcomes as a result.

In this chapter, I want to explore three fundamental myths about stress. The key to flourishing at work comes from seeing through these misperceptions.

1. Life is stressful.

2. Negative feelings are a signal that something is wrong.

3. Stress can be healthy and motivating.

Myth No. 1: Life is stressful

On a BBC breakfast news show, ex-basketball player and psychologist John Amaechi and Iain O'Brien, an ex-cricketer (who suffered with depression), were being interviewed about Jonathan Trott's departure from cricket.[3]

'Are there some sports that are just more stressful than others?' the interviewer asked. John Amaechi responded by explaining that there are many people in all walks of life who are suffering the same type of crisis as Trott. He went on to say that the cause of Trott's stress was not cricket. 'But is there something about cricket perhaps?' the interviewer persisted, giving reasons why cricket is more pressurised than other sports.

The interviewer's line of questioning highlights a pervasive and widespread misperception.

Whether it's their workload, the boss or the traffic, it's extremely common to hear people describing situations or circumstances as being inherently stressful. In my research this belief came through loud and clear.

Top four reasons why workers say they feel stressed, anxious or worried at work are:

1. Workload (66%)
2. Pressure of deadlines (53%)
3. Not enough time (46%)
4. Other people/relationship issues (34%)

'My own thinking/mindset' was ranked 9th out of 10 with 18%.

Once again we see strong evidence of the misunderstanding that exists when it comes to the experience of stress. The crucial connection between how we think and how we feel is either invisible or misunderstood by many of us. And it's made less visible by the plethora of people telling us that life is stressful.

For example, on the stress.org.uk website, it says:

> 'We live in a stressful era, possibly the most stressful period humans have ever experienced. It is the biggest issue that modern man has to deal with and the biggest cause of illness some of which even lead to death. It is the issue that costs companies and our economies billions.'[4]

As well as the stress industry itself, there are thousands of books and websites authored by well-meaning consultants, psychologists and 'stress' experts who describe the multitude of 'stressors' in life. They tell us that we cannot possibly eliminate stress because there are just too many sources of anxiety that are out of our control. We're advised that the best we can do is learn to manage ourselves and life's circumstances better.

We're offered tricks, tips and coping strategies. We're prescribed everything from gratitude journals and raw diets to meditation or affirmations. We're told to think positive, do more exercise, be more socially active or get more sleep. This is all well and good but for many, seeing the positive or being sociable, is the last thing people want to do when they are feeling low or anxious.

Therapies and techniques such as Mindfulness and Cognitive Behavioural Therapy (CBT) are also designed to tame our anxious minds and make our lives less stressful.

While many of these strategies may be helpful in the short term, they still serve to perpetuate the mistaken belief that something other than our own thinking can make us feel stressed or anxious. They innocently point us in the wrong direction.

My aim in this chapter is to show why the *No.1* reason for feeling stressed or anxious (and dare I say the only reason) is our own thinking, shaped by our understanding of the inside-out nature of life.

There is no doubt that the *experience* of stress and anxiety exists. Physical symptoms from fatigue, eczema, headaches and high blood pressure to a complete meltdown of the immune system are evidence of this. Many physical illnesses have been linked to stress. There are also many psychological symptoms including insomnia, irritability, lack of patience, sadness, apathy, depression. The list goes on.

In order to understand how stress really works, it's useful to first consider it from a biological perspective.

As a species, we've evolved over thousands of years to handle genuinely life-threatening situations. In these scenarios, the arousal (stress) hormones are activated and a biological process commonly known as *fight or flight* kicks in.

The system does its job by instigating a range of physiological changes to protect us. Adrenaline is pumped into the bloodstream. The heart beats faster than normal. Blood pressure and pulse rate increases. Breathing often speeds up. With each breath, the lungs are able to take in more oxygen. We become more alert as our senses sharpen. Glucose and cholesterol flood into the bloodstream. This 'threat response' happens incredibly fast because it's designed to sharpen our responses, to get us out of danger and keep us safe.

Whilst this intelligent process was designed to save us from the proverbial sabre-toothed tiger, many people are activating this 'threat response' several times a day – not when their life is on the line but when their ego is on the line! It wasn't designed for a bad day at the office – unless your office happens to be in the middle of a jungle or warzone.

In addition, this threat response was intended to last a matter of minutes, yet many of us are living in this high-arousal state for many hours each day and it takes its toll – as indicated by all the symptoms described above.

After a prolonged period of high arousal, cortisol is released into the bloodstream, which keeps us in a high-alert state. Our minds and bodies simply aren't designed to endure the impact of this chronic stress state, which is known to cause many health issues including high blood pressure and increased risk of heart attacks.

> **The secret to psychological wellbeing and optimal performance is to understand what triggers this 'stress response' and what keeps us there. So far, all the evidence points to *Thought and perception* as the primary cause.**

What if stress isn't just a fact of life?

The outside-in belief – that our feelings can come from something other than Thought in the moment – is ingrained in the human psyche. For example, moving house is often cited as one of the most stressful things a person can do, but any experience of struggle or stress during a house move can only come from one place – the thinking that you're having about the situation and the feelings your thinking creates.

I frequently travel by plane. During severe turbulence I've been known to grab the arm of the poor unsuspecting passenger sitting beside me. On a particularly bumpy flight en route to Tokyo, I could feel my heart race and the panic rise. Talk about fight or flight!

I remember looking at the other passengers and I was struck by how relaxed and calm everyone seemed. There were people quite happily tucking into their dinner. Some were fast asleep while others were chatting and laughing. I was surprised that no one else looked worried. I saw no signs of panic or anxiety. Maybe they were distracted from the turbulence because they were busy doing other things.

In that moment, I had a powerful realisation that my experience of panic was made of Thought. It had nothing to do with the turbulence. It had nothing to do with the plane journey. I was sitting there, experiencing the feelings that my thinking was giving me.

I saw with total clarity that I too could feel peaceful like the lady next to me. My thoughts of crashing, leaving my family behind and other helpful images were giving rise to my panicky feelings. I hadn't made that connection between my thoughts and feelings.

We look outside ourselves for an answer to something that is being created on the inside.

As soon as I realised where my fear and anxiety was coming from, it landed me back into the present moment. I felt an instant sense of calm wash over me. Regardless of how bumpy the ride was, I knew I was OK.

I'm not saying that I now love bumpy plane rides because I don't. But knowing that any feelings of panic and fear are a temporary response to some passing thoughts is very helpful. It allows you to move through any experience more gracefully. It takes a lot of unnecessary thinking off your mind. And in my case, my fellow passengers don't have to put up with being grabbed by a panicky passenger!

In the BBC studio, the interviewer continued to blame the pressure of cricket for Trott's departure. O'Brien offered a solution – change the way we interact *with ourselves*. I agree with this but I'd like to take it a step further.

In order to truly flourish and experience life without unnecessary suffering, we need insight into how Thought works. This helps us to be less hoodwinked by our own thinking.

The principles of Mind, Thought and Consciousness provide a logic that shows us how:

- We experience our personal realities through Thought, moment to moment.

- We live in the feelings that our thinking creates.

- We have infinite potential for new thinking in any moment, which instantly creates a new experience of reality.

Despite being told there are many external 'stressors' causing our internal suffering, doctors have been unable to find any consistency in what stresses one person versus another. This is because the experience of stress doesn't exist *out there* in the world. There is nothing outside of us (separate to us) that's *inherently stressful*. It's always a function of how we are thinking, feeling and consequently perceiving situations. And how we are thinking about something is not determined by what's going on around us.

My first response when I heard this was 'how can the situation have *nothing* to do with how I am thinking? It must have *some* influence'.

Most people will insist that if not for their high-pressure job, demanding clients or screaming kids, they wouldn't be thinking that way in the first place. This was certainly how I used to see it. So let's take a closer look and I'll share some examples as you reflect on your own experiences.

If the workload causes our stress – as many people believe – then a team with the same workload would surely all find it stressful, but this is rarely the case. Instead what we find is a variety of different perceptions and experiences of the same external demands.

And if it were the pressure of deadlines, then why do some people thrive with deadlines whilst others have a total meltdown?

I have colleagues who, by their own admission, have easy lives, yet they're constantly worrying or feeling anxious. I know other people who have very challenging and busy lives and live in a high level of wellbeing and contentment.

If the cricket was causing the player to feel stressed, then why doesn't every cricketer (at the same game) get overwhelmed or anxious and have to bail out?

All around us we see evidence of the inside-out truth and the illusion of the outside-in.

> **We have a thought and we put it outside of ourselves. We project our thoughts onto a situation, a person, a past or future event and then we forget that it's Thought. It becomes part of a fixed reality out there, outside of us.**

Consciousness makes our Thought-generated experience look and feel so real that our feelings must surely be coming from somewhere other than our own thinking.

Here's the belief that most people subscribe to:

Person/future event/past event/current situation makes me [stressed/anxious] = my current state of mind (how I think and feel)

Outside-in

This outside-in belief implies that your feelings can come from somewhere other than Thought. So perhaps you agree with 18% of people in my research who chose 'my own thinking or mindset' as having something to do with their experience of stress, anxiety or worry?

In my study, I also asked people for their view on the statement

"Stress comes from how people think and not from the circumstances". I wanted to check if we'd see a different result by asking a different question. We did.

55% of people agree that 'Stress comes from how people think and not from the circumstances'. Of those people, only 7% *strongly agree*.

45% disagree that stress comes from how people think.

This finding reveals that sometimes we believe that our feelings of stress, anxiety or worry come from the circumstances and sometimes it comes from our own thinking.

Here's an updated formula that reflects this:

[outside factor] i.e. something other than my own thinking + my own thinking = my state of mind (how I think and feel)

As we explored in Chapter 3, this is an example of a mixed paradigm understanding.

Here is how stress works:

We have some thinking.

We believe the feelings arising from Thought can be caused by something other than our own thinking.

This thought makes us feel 'at effect' of something outside of us (other people, situations, past events, future scenarios).

This fills our head with 'stressful' thoughts of how to manage, handle or control all these things 'out there' that we believe are causing our stressful experience.

The result is a congested, speedy or anxious state of mind.

Inside-out

The logic of the principles reveals to us that outside factors have no inherent meaning in and of themselves. All that exists 'outside' of us is sensory data. We create our personal experience of 'stressful' by how we use Thought.

How we *think* stress works determines how we experience it.

> ## YES BUT...
>
> What if someone is being bullied or abused – are you saying that's just their thinking?

The principles aren't a way of negating unacceptable or inhumane behaviour. Every day, people are dealing with extremely difficult situations by anyone's standards.

The human operating principles provide an unbending logic that explains how all feelings – including fear, guilt, jealousy or anxiety – are created by how we are thinking in any given moment. How those feelings affect you is a direct result of your understanding and recognition of how the system works.

I have clients who are senior social workers. Social care is recognised as a highly stressful and challenging sector. The work involves supporting people who are dealing with a number of issues including homelessness, addiction, abuse and mental health problems. They have to remove children from families and make decisions that change people's lives. One of the biggest benefits they get from learning about these principles is increased mental clarity and the ability to keep their bearings in challenging situations. It allows them to listen without prejudice, connect more deeply with people and bring wiser, more balanced thinking to decisions and actions.

Whether we see the truth or not, it doesn't change the fact of how Thought works. That's the nature of principles and there's something very solid and reliable about that. Whilst we may innocently misunderstand how the mind works, it just does its thing until we catch on.

David's story

David is a project leader who was experiencing extreme levels of stress and bordering on burnout.

At the end of each working day, he would go home and need a couple of hours to calm down before he could properly engage with his wife. He was working around the clock and found it impossible to switch off and relax. He'd stopped doing things he enjoyed such as bike rides and other hobbies.

His self-confidence at work was low and his relationships with some of his colleagues were strained. His mind was so busy that he wasn't able to express himself clearly in meetings and conversations. His lack of clarity reduced his leadership impact with colleagues.

David couldn't see any possibility of feeling better unless the situation at work changed. He was deeply unhappy and was questioning whether he was in the right role. Leaving the job seemed like the best and only solution.

How do you know if you're seeing a situation with clarity and perspective if your mind is full of anxiety or worry? It's hard to make good decisions in that state of mind.

Here's what David realised and how it took him from burnout to brilliant.

1. 'MY THINKING IS CREATING MY STRESS'

Like most people, David believed that his state of mind was the result of his increasing workload, other people and the complexity and timelines of the project. From this outside-in perspective, every demand or request that was made (whether in his work or personal life) was another reason to feel more even stressed out. This caused him to avoid certain meetings or calls. These choices and behaviours were David's coping mechanisms but they created more problems. Work piled up and people became frustrated with his lack of responsiveness.

2. 'I'M FEELING MY THINKING'

Like most of us, David thought his feelings were a response to other people and the job itself. Because of this, he believed the only way he could feel better was if the situation changed.

He put a lot of energy into trying to control, manage or manipulate the situation in the hope that it would improve and, in turn, make him feel better. This generated more thinking and effort which created more anxiety and reinforced his outside-in belief.

As soon as David learnt that nothing could make him feel that way except for his own thoughts, he felt very different. Annoying colleagues began to look like 'annoying thinking'. A lot of the urgency began to look like 'urgent thinking' rather than genuine urgency *out there*. He realised it was his own perceptions that made his work life appear so overwhelming. He had thought it was the other way round.

As David became more aware (in the moment) of the source of his feelings, a lot of his old thinking was rendered irrelevant. As a result he began to regain more clarity and confidence.

3. 'I DON'T HAVE TO THINK ABOUT EVERY THOUGHT I HAVE'

David didn't realise that he could choose which thoughts to engage with and which ones to ignore.

Before he learnt about the nature of Thought, if he felt stressed he would take his thinking very seriously. He would engage with every thought he had and question, scrutinise and chew over them. By doing that, he was quite literally breathing more life into his thinking, which made it look more real to him.

As David gained more understanding, he began to hold his thoughts more lightly. Rather than grabbing onto every thought, he began to relate to them as just 'temporary unwanted visitors' that he could ignore if he chose to.

In his words:

> 'It definitely turned around certain aspects of the job where I really thought I'd had it and I didn't want to follow that course any longer. But actually when I took away some of the noise, I found that I was enjoying work... even the busy days could be enjoyable because I was looking at them in a very different way. I think the biggest initial change for me was finding that I had more time in my day, having that clear mind... taking the noise out of my head just gave me that spare capacity. That's what made me more productive.

> 'I think the second thing was learning how to reset. When my workday finished I actually got on with my life. I found I had time to do the things that I had just stopped doing.'

Thoughts might knock on the door and sometimes they find their way in without your permission. Innocently, we give them the best seat in the house. We feed them our finest food and invite them to stay the night. We say it's OK for all their friends to pop round too. Before you know it, the 'mind-house' is full!

> 68% of people say that when things go wrong at work, they tend to ruminate or dwell on them for a long time afterwards.

This has some important implications in terms of our enjoyment of work and our quality of performance.

Have you ever spent the morning lost in thought about a situation that went wrong or worrying about a conversation you need to have in the future?

In June 2011, the BBC conducted one of the largest ever studies into stress.

The early summary of the research said: *'Ruminating* – or dwelling too long on negative events – was the biggest predictor of mental health problems.'[5]

As we've explored, Thought is often invisible to us. We think as naturally as we breathe. Often, we don't realise we've been recycling the same thoughts over and over again until either we get distracted or we become aware of how we're feeling or thinking.

For every human being, Thought is always instantly expressed as a feeling, including chemical reactions in our system. It's our understanding and recognition of this, in any given moment, that determines how quickly we bounce back and regain our mental clarity.

The one and only thing that gets us into trouble and keeps us stuck in stressful, anxious or worried states of mind is how we innocently split Thought and feeling through the mistaken belief that our feelings can be caused by something other than our own thinking – e.g. the boss, workload, weather, lack of money.

In David's case, when he re-gained his mental clarity and got new perspectives about his work life, he began to enjoy his job and feel motivated and engaged again. Where the workload really was unrealistic, he had the clarity to deal with it effectively. For example, he was able to make a strong case to the management team to reduce the workload and he came up with solutions that worked for him and for the wider team.

This won't be the case for everyone. For some of us, there will be issues at work that we may decide are unacceptable or intolerable. Once again, your clarity of mind and common sense will guide you to make the right choices and decisions. This could mean leaving a job, making a complaint, seeking advice or challenging the status quo.

Your understanding and recognition of the Thought–Feeling partnership, will always bring you back to your natural clarity.

If my thinking is the problem, how do I change it?

I was sitting with a client and we were discussing state of mind. She'd had some realisations and I wanted to find out what she was noticing. Here's the conversation verbatim:

CLIENT   I've noticed just how much 'negative' thinking and worrying I do on a daily basis. I can't believe it. No wonder I've been feeling so anxious. How do I change my thinking?

ME   Have you tried to change your thinking?

CLIENT   Yes it's bloody hard work!

ME   It's probably like having a second job isn't it?

[lots of laughing]

ME   So I'm curious. Why were you trying to change your thinking?

CLIENT   Because now I know it's my own thinking that's making me feel bad, so if I can stop thinking those thoughts and have more positive thoughts, I will feel better and then I'll do a better job.

Let's explore this further...

As you begin to look more in this direction, the role of thought in your experience will become much more visible to you. You might find yourself becoming more aware of the volume or speed of thought. You'll also find that you become more conscious of the direct connection between your thoughts and your feelings.

Most personal development approaches are based on some form of 'positive thinking'. They are built on the premise that we can manifest or attract better outcomes by thinking more positively. However many times I think about winning the lottery, I still haven't managed to manifest it.

Another popular approach is Cognitive Behavioural Therapy (CBT). Whilst it does connect thoughts to feelings, it's still based on an *outside-in* model of life. The premise is that something outside of our own thinking can generate our internal experience. As such we're encouraged to generate better or more helpful thoughts *about the circumstances*. But the focus is still on the *personal content of thought* rather than on the *impersonal* and universal *nature of Thought itself*.

I've discovered over the past few years that there are some pitfalls with these cognitive approaches. The first is that they teach us (directly or indirectly) that if we have 'better' or more positive thoughts we'll be happier and more successful. Negative thoughts are bad and positive thoughts are good. So we're encouraged to monitor and manage our thinking and cultivate a positive mindset.

There is nothing wrong with the deeper intention behind these approaches. Living in a more positive and hopeful feeling helps us to flourish and enjoy life. But not if we're deluding ourselves. Let me give you an example.

Several years ago I was facilitating a training session about influence. The group was practising a technique called 're-framing'. The idea is to take a topic, issue or perceived problem and then put a variety of different 'frames' around the issue in order to generate new and different perspectives.

For example, let's say you were angry because someone at work was behaving in an aggressive way towards you and it was bothering you. A reframe might involve asking yourself questions such as:

- What else could their behaviour mean?

- In what context would this behaviour be appropriate?

- How might other people view this behaviour?

One of the participants was exploring a difficulty she was having with a colleague at work. She called me over to say that she was struggling with the exercise. When I asked her why, she said: 'I can't trick myself into thinking that I'm OK with what they did. It doesn't change how I feel.'

This is a great example of what happens when we focus on the content of thought rather than on how Thought works.

When we change the content of our thinking we are swopping one thought for another. You can think of this as a horizontal change – a change that occurs at the same level of thinking that created it. For example, "Maybe he didn't mean that. Maybe he meant this". As Einstein famously said "We cannot solve our problems with the same thinking that created them".

Swopping one belief or story for another is an example of trying to solve an issue at the same level of understanding that created the feeling in the first place.

My client was attributing her upset feelings to the other person's behaviour. No matter how many different 'stories' or re-frames she created, she would still walk away believing that something other than her own thinking had the power to make her feel a particular way.

Understanding the nature of Thought (how thought works), is a *vertical* change.

When you insightfully see how *all experience, all feelings* are being created by the same universal, formless principles, it generates a spontaneous shift in consciousness where you're able to see life from a more objective, less personal vantage point. From this new perspective, you realise that it's not about good thinking–bad thinking. *It's all Thought.* All the way up and all the way down.

Focus on Content versus Focus on the Nature of Thought

The wonderful thing about realising the inside-out nature of life is that we no longer have to work on our thinking or change it in order to get clarity or feel calmer and less anxious. It's much simpler than that. Let me explain this in a different way by using TV and movies as examples.

When I was young, like many children I had a vivid imagination and I didn't know how TV worked. I thought what I was watching on the screen was real. When I got scared, my mum would calm me down by saying: 'It's just a TV programme. It's not real. There are camera men behind the scenes and microphones hanging down.' She helped me understand how TV works so I could enjoy the entertainment without being hoodwinked by the perceived reality of it.

When you know how movies work, you can watch anything, however scary, without having to constantly remind yourself that it's just a movie. You don't have to grab a weapon or change the channel because you know it's not real.

In the same way, when you understand how Thought works, you don't have to change your thinking or put a better spin on it in order to feel better or clear your mind. You can realise in any moment that what you're feeling is Thought which means it can't harm you.

Movies are also a brilliant demonstration of where our feelings come from and how we relate to them. We watch actors on a screen, a play of light – none of it real – and yet we cry, scream, laugh or get annoyed. We go on a rollercoaster ride of emotions. We want to feel scared, sad, intrigued or angry. It's all part of the experience of watching a movie. Wouldn't you feel cheated if the scary movie didn't make you jump or the thriller left you yawning?

Rollercoasters are a great example of how we can enjoy the full range of emotions that our thinking gives us. And it's this range of feelings or emotions that makes us human.

Feelings are like ice-cream. It comes in different flavours – chocolate, strawberry, vanilla, butterscotch. Some flavours we like and others we don't, but ultimately they're all ice-cream.

In the same way, we experience the various flavours of feelings. We call them sad, happy, excited, inspired, annoyed, scared. We like some and we don't like others. But ultimately, they are all flavours of Thought. They have no inherent power over us because they are forms of energy moving through us. And behind all those passing flavours of Thought is a natural, unchanging state of pure clarity and wellbeing.

These operating principles are the ultimate movie makers. Thought is the best creative director in the world and Consciousness is the best special effects director. As we gain more understanding of how they work together, using the power of Mind to create our personal experience of reality, we can live life with more grace and ease and less stress.

> 'All feelings derive and become alive, whether negative or positive, from the power of Thought'[6]
>
> **SYDNEY BANKS**

So now on to the next myth – what our feelings *mean*.

Myth No.2: Negative feelings are a signal that something is wrong

One of the most commonly held beliefs is that our feelings are telling us something about our life, when as we've explored so far, they are telling us about our thinking.

Our feelings are the single most important indicator in this beautifully intelligent system that we've been gifted. They play a pivotal part in the human operating system. In the same way that physical pain is vital feedback about our bodies, our feelings or emotions alert us to Thought in the moment.

The human dashboard

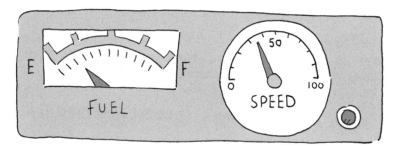

As a car driver, the gauges and lights on the dashboard are important. They provide vital information that lets you know what's going on inside the car.

The speedometer lets you know when to slow down or stop. When the fuel tank is empty, the gauge lights up to let you know you need to re-fill the tank. If you ignore the warning sign, you'll end up stuck somewhere and unable to drive the car. This crucial feedback is designed to help and guide you. Imagine driving a car that has no fuel gauge.

Just like the fuel gauge, your feelings are there to give you valuable feedback and signals about what's going on inside you.

When we understand the signals and what they mean, we can use them effectively. If we misread them, we might innocently make things worse for ourselves or others.

Any anxious, stressful or worried feelings are the 'light' coming on. Our feelings let us know that we're experiencing our own thinking.

Before I had some understanding of these principles, I would take my low moods or anxious feelings as a sign that something was wrong with me or with the world. If I felt irritable, I would start to wonder what was causing it. The most obvious direction to look was outside. When we look out there we will always find reasons and justifications for our feelings. The more you look outside for the solution to your state of mind, the more thinking it will create and the more your clarity will be compromised.

Our feelings are like a temporary weather system moving through us. We don't have to take our thoughts or feelings seriously just as we don't have to take a cloudy day seriously.

At any moment, we can have a new and wiser thought about our experience which automatically shifts our consciousness. In an instant, we can see life in a brand new way. That's what one fresh thought can do for you.

When you know that feelings are Thought taking form in the moment, you can be in any feeling state without it dominating or controlling you.

How do you know whether to trust your thinking?

Have you ever stopped yourself from making a phone call or delayed sending an email because you knew your head wasn't in the right place?

We tell each other to 'sleep on it' before we make important decisions because we know that tomorrow things may look very different – that we can feel different. The nature of Thought is such that we can have a change of thinking and a change of heart at any moment. But we can't control that, just as we can't control the tides.

Do you know what thought you will have next? If you could know, then surely you'd put in a request for 'only wise or happy thoughts please' or whatever your preference might be. While your next thought is unpredictable, your innate wisdom and common sense is always available. It's built into the intelligence of the system and sometimes we listen to it and other times we override it.

The answer to reducing anxious or stressful feelings is not to analyse the situation or dissect your thinking.

If you ask a thought whether it's credible or not, it's going to tell you it is! Our thinking always sets out to prove itself to be true. Thought is incredibly deceptive. It's self-validating and that's why we need a more reliable way to navigate our experience of life. We have to go beyond our thinking... and move to a higher, more objective vantage point.

And that's where your feeling state is really helpful. It's a trusted guide, a trusted companion that lets you know that you may not be seeing things with clarity and perspective. It's the light on the dashboard warning you to slow down or stop. It's the logic and wisdom of the system expressing itself through you.

In any given moment, where do you think your feelings are coming from?

In any moment of struggle or difficulty, seeing the answer to this question, will help to guide you back to the present moment – back to clarity.

So now on to the third and final myth about stress.

Myth No.3: Stress can be motivating/stress can be healthy

In the early days of my career in sales and management, I operated in first gear much of the time. I had a lot of energy, passion and enthusiasm but I also had a fair amount of anxiety. I thought this was a natural or inevitable part of being passionate and driven at work. Many people seem to operate this way.

76% of workers agree that stress, anxiety and worry is a natural or inevitable part of work life.

To the degree that you see that stress is thought and that thought is a natural aspect of being human, then stress is a natural part of work life. However, the suffering that we experience is not inevitable. That's something we can change by understanding how Thought works.

I've worked with many clients who believed that stress was a good source of motivation but this too is part of the misperception.

When you're doing your best work, how would you describe your state of mind in those moments? It's unlikely that you'd say you were anxious and stressed out.

I'm not saying that we can't function if we're feeling stressed or anxious. It's really a matter of *how well* we function and the costs or impact of working in that state of mind. I've yet to meet anyone who agrees that they perform better when they are feeling stressed, worried or anxious. What you tend to find are people taking action or making decisions based on distorted or unreliable thinking.

There is no such thing as healthy stress but there is a healthy and optimal state of mind. We each have an unlimited and unconditional source of wellbeing or clarity that helps us do our best work.

There is no good or bad stress because stress doesn't exist as an independent experience beyond our own thinking. There are feelings that we experience and respond to that are created by our own thinking.

When someone says that they feel stressed or that something is stressful, they are describing their thought-created perception of a situation. Our entire relationship with life is via Thought first and foremost.

Under pressure

Would you describe yourself as someone who works well under pressure? Do you like the adrenalin of a last minute rush to get something finished? Or do you prefer to plan intensively and avoid that last minute rush?

On the HSE website, it says:

> 'There is a difference between pressure and stress. Pressure can be positive and a motivating factor, and is often essential in a job. It can help us achieve our goals and perform better. Stress occurs when this pressure becomes excessive. Stress is a natural reaction to too much pressure.'[7]

Whilst they are talked about as two different things, stress and pressure *are the same thing*. They are both experiences of Thought which create particular feelings. It's how we relate to those feelings that dictates our experience of any situation.

YES BUT...

'What if I am given a day to complete a really important job at work and there's a lot riding on it? That's pressure'

You might have targets, tasks or deadlines that you have to meet, in which case you could say there are external demands. But how you experience those demands is 100% up to how you think about them and consequently how you perceive and experience them.

One person's challenge is another person's breaking point.

To more gracefully ride the waves of life it's incredibly helpful to understand how the human operating system works and where our feelings come from. This perspective and a deeper understanding is what allows each of us to transcend our own thinking and thrive regardless of what is happening around us or to us.

There is no doubt that people are dealing with extremely difficult situations at work every day. There's no denying that bereavement, abuse, earthquakes and wars can be scary, traumatic or devastating for many people. But it's also liberating to realise that *all* emotional suffering can only ever come from our moment to moment thinking and that we have innate resilience and wisdom to deal with whatever life throws at us.

Thought is a transient experience which means all feelings of stress and anxiety are also temporary in nature. This fact alone has the power to free people from their mental shackles, taking them from a passive, out of control feeling, to a more hopeful, empowered feeling.

Mental clarity and wellbeing is always there behind your passing thoughts, just as blue sky is always there behind the clouds. You can always rely on that even in the worst weather conditions.

In essence

- There is nothing *outside of us* that is inherently stressful. We can only experience outside via Thought.

- We cannot experience something as *stressful* or *worrying* if we don't first think it.

- Anxious feelings are telling us about our thinking, not about our lives.

- It's not about good thinking-bad thinking. *It's all thought.*

- Mental clarity (a clear and free mind) is our natural or 'default' state.

Part 2

Uncovering the truth about what it takes to excel at work

Chapter 5

The Performance Placebo
Mind over matter

'Nothing is so difficult as not deceiving oneself.'

Ludwig Wittgenstein

Human beings are brilliant learners. It's often said that we learn more in the first seven years of our lives than we do in the rest of our lives. As babies, we're like sponges absorbing all that we see, hear and experience. We master complex skills, learning to walk and talk. We model how other people think and behave.

As impressionable youngsters, we take on the ideas and opinions of those we look up to – parental figures, teachers, friends. These thoughts that we've acquired and collected become beliefs or rules that unconsciously shape and direct our choices and actions. Some are learned fast, via a specific event. For example, someone has a car accident and in a split second they decide that 'fast is dangerous', and in an instant, they've created a rule about driving slowly. They may even create an additional rule about slowing down in life.

Other beliefs are learned gradually through time perhaps through a parent or an authority figure. For example, I worked with a manager who wanted to improve his relationships with staff. He was newly appointed and his style of management was proving to be de-motivating for his team so I was called in to help him make some adjustments.

As we talked he told me that one of his team wasn't passionate or committed to the job.

'How do you know that?' I asked.

'She gets in on the dot of 9am and leaves at 5pm.'

'I don't understand. How does that mean that she's not passionate or committed?' I was curious to understand his logic.

'Because if she was really committed, she would come in early and stay late like I do.'

He started to share his ideas about what it meant to be committed to a job. He revealed that he often got in early and most days he stayed late. As we reflected together, he remembered that his father used to tell him: 'If you're committed to something, you work hard and put in the extra hours.' His father had spent much of his life working. Unbeknownst to him, my client had internalised his father's belief and it had guided his approach to work ever since.

As soon as he saw it for what it was – an old thought – it no longer made sense to hold on to it. There was nothing he had to do. In an instant, it became irrelevant and his behaviour and management style changed in line with his fresh perspective.

Many of the rules we learn or create are vital for safely navigating the physical world. Learning that we can burn unprotected hands on a hot stove is a good rule to live by. Learning to stop at a red traffic light is a useful habit if you're a driver.

In fact I recently found myself stopping at a red traffic light only to realise that I was *on the pavement* next to a line of traffic as I *walked* to my local shops. As soon as I became conscious of my mistake, I stood and laughed at what I'd done, marvelling at the sheer power of thought and conditioning.

As we travel through life collecting various ideas, we learn to think in particular ways about ourselves, about others and about life. Those 'hand me down' thoughts become like truths that we hold on to, often unknowingly. While they may be hidden from our view, they guide and shape our thinking and behaviour.

When I was growing up, my mum was a single parent for a while and she worked hard to earn a living to provide for my sister and me. She had strong beliefs about money and independence and to guide me through life, she was keen to pass her beliefs on to me.

It wasn't until I was older that I realised how some of my mum's ideas had become part of my reality, part of my truth about how life works. I had confused fact with fiction.

> **Fact** – there is something called money. There is something called independence.

> **Fiction** – everything we think about money and everything we think about independence.

The reason thoughts are called beliefs is simply because we often relate to them as truths or facts.

> 'Belief is not the beginning of knowledge, but the end.'
>
> **GOETHE**

All ideas, opinions, judgements and beliefs are Thought. Anything we can conceive in our minds – all mental activity – is the principle of Thought taking form moment to moment.

Individual thoughts occur. We connect some thoughts while others just disappear into the ether. Beliefs are just a system of interconnected thoughts.

Those collected and connected thoughts become part of a 'personal thought system' creating our outlook or world-view.

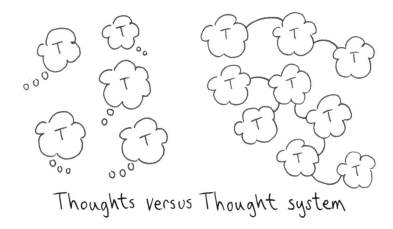

Thoughts versus Thought system

When you recognise in any moment that your opinions, judgements and beliefs are just thoughts that you've subscribed to, you can choose to un-subscribe. It's only your attachment to any particular thought that keeps it alive and generates the feelings, behaviours and actions that result from any particular thinking.

I've unsubscribed to many ideas and beliefs and some I've chosen to hold on to. For example, I believe that people inherently want to do the right thing. Sometimes, their behaviour may demonstrate otherwise, but I see this as a temporary loss of perspective or lack of clarity on their part. This has been a helpful way to think about others. Rather than see my belief as a fundamental truth, I know it's a thought – an idea that I have about people. The only truth of which I am sure is that I'm a thinker and I use Thought to generate ideas about the world and to create my subjective experience of reality.

Cultures, communities and societies are built on and led by people's belief (thought) systems.

As motivating and helpful as our thoughts can be, our ideas about ourselves or the world can also limit our experience. You often hear people say things like 'change takes time' or 'people don't like change'. There are many ideas like this that we accept as true. These beliefs can narrow our focus, reducing possibility. And it's not just the ideas or beliefs we have about ourselves. The beliefs that others have about us can also have a major impact if we don't distinguish them as Thought.

In a classic experiment in 1968, Robert Rosenthal's study highlighted the impact of thought when it comes to learning.

A group of students were given a standard IQ test. The results were scored and the researchers told the teachers that five students in the class had unusually high IQ scores and were likely to surpass their classmates during the rest of the term. Those five 'high-score' students were in fact picked at random. They were no more gifted than any other student. By the end of the school year, all the students had gained in IQ but the five 'chosen' students had increased their scores significantly more than the others.

The teachers' attitudes about their students affected how they taught them. This seemed to have a very tangible and positive impact on the performance of the 'gifted' students.[1]

Thought – the ultimate performance placebo

Whilst pain is physical, it's often described by doctors as a psychological experience. We have pain receptors but Thought and Consciousness are the activating agents in our actual experience of pain.

In 2006, the More4 TV channel broadcast a live hernia operation successfully performed on a hypnotised patient *without a general anaesthetic*.[2]

If you had any doubt about the power of the mind, this example is fascinating. His heart rate and vital signs were consistent with what surgeons would expect if the patient were under a general anaesthetic. When the surgery was complete, the patient was brought out of hypnosis, he got up and talked to the team as if he'd just been shopping for groceries.

Jack Gibson was the surgeon who pioneered 'hypno-surgery' as early as the 1950s. Using the power of the patient's mind through hypnosis, he removed a blood clot from behind a patient's eye without any anaesthetic.[3] You could tell from some graphic footage that the patient had experienced no pain whatsoever during the procedure. Gibson reputedly performed around 4000 surgeries in this way – without any pain relief.

Mind over matter is more than just a popular saying and the placebo effect is a great example of this.

In a UK TV show called *Fear and Faith*, Derren Brown brought together a group of people who had unwanted phobias.[4] They believed they were trialling a new wonder drug to cure them of their fears. Derren invited them to a clinic (a set) with a professor and clinician (an actor) who introduced them to the new drug called Rumyodin (a sugar pill).

Nick had a disabling fear of confrontation. Katie had a fear of singing in public but wanted to be a stage singer. Daniel had a phobia of heights that included walking across any type of bridge. Within a few days of taking the sugar pill, they each started to show some positive changes.

After a few weeks and in the final dramatic scene, Derren took Daniel across a very high bridge. Not only did Daniel walk across it, but he sat down on a ledge with Derren, dangling his feet over the high drop. Then the big reveal: Derren told Daniel that the wonder drug was actually just a sugar pill. Daniel's response was that he felt even better because he had overcome the phobia himself through his own mind.

Derren later revealed to participants that Rumyodin was an anagram of Your Mind.

There are many fascinating studies on how the placebo effect still works even when people are told that it's a placebo!

For a BBC *Horizon* documentary, they set out to test some assumptions about placebo. One of the assumptions is that in order for placebo to work, a person has to be 'tricked' and told they are taking a genuine drug as opposed to a sugar pill.[5]

One woman who took part in the trial had been experiencing very severe IBS. She described her symptoms as being so bad that she didn't want to leave home, even to go shopping. She was recruited along with 80 other 'sufferers' onto the trial. She was told she would be taking a placebo with no active ingredient but that 'they might work thanks to your own self-healing processes'. She openly stated that she wasn't convinced it could work but she took the placebo.

After three days of taking the sugar pill, she realised she was no longer in pain and all severe symptoms had gone. She wasn't the only one who experienced positive results: 62% of those on the trial said they got 'adequate relief' from taking the placebo.

The placebo effect is a clear demonstration of the sheer power of Thought and its relationship with our mind and body. Placebo is thought.

In 1979, a ground-breaking experiment was carried out by psychologist Ellen Langer to find out the link between thought and the ageing process.[6]

Professor Langer recruited a group of elderly men, all in their 70s and 80s. They were told they were going to have a 'week of reminiscence and nostalgia'. They didn't know it was a study about ageing.

Langer wanted to find out how taking these men back 20 years would impact on their bodies.

They were taken to a retreat site and split into two groups. The experimental group would be talking about life in the 1950s, surrounded by props to create a 50s environment. They were asked to act as if it were 1959. The control group stayed in their current era.

The retreat site had no 'age'-related equipment such as handrails or other special aids. When they arrived at the retreat the men were asked to carry their own bags into their temporary abode – even if that meant taking one item in at a time.

It wasn't long before these men were acting differently. Langer noticed they were steadier on their feet, more confident and one man stopped using his walking stick.

The pre and post tests showed some significant changes, including a drop in blood pressure and even improvements in eyesight and hearing!

Whilst both groups showed changes, it was the experimental group that showed the biggest change.

This fascinating experiment points to the relationship between Thought, self-perception and behaviour.

Bruce Lipton is a cellular biologist and author of *The Biology of Belief*[7] and *Spontaneous Evolution*[7]. His fascinating work sheds light on the role of thought in our genetic make-up and our behaviour.

The traditional understanding is that our genes (DNA) control us, but what Lipton's ground breaking research revealed is how Thought influences and changes genes.

Genetic predisposition is often cited as the cause of certain behaviours, mental illnesses or even personality traits, which implies that they are unchangeable. Lipton's research is a game changer. He says 'The bottom line is that the genes do not control biology. This is a mistake. This is an assumption'. His research indicates that it's the cell that affects the environment and not the environment that affects the cell.

His work was perceived as radical and dismissed by many, but now the field of epigenetics has become the cutting edge of genetic science, showing us how thought can alter our gene expression. What this means is that we are not controlled by our genetic makeup. Research is showing how thoughts can switch genes on and off.

In January 2011, *Time* Magazine's front cover headline was 'Why your DNA isn't your Destiny'.[8] The article talks about how the choices we make can change our genes.

In a recorded interview, Bruce Lipton says the following[9]:

> **The brain is like a chemist. The brain secretes the chemistry into the blood that changes the fate of the cells. But the brain doesn't do this automatically. It does it in connection with our mind, our beliefs, and our perceptions.**

> So if you're afraid – for example, if you live in fear, you're releasing stress hormones into the culture medium (the blood) and that changes the fate of the cells as they get into protection. Or if you're living in love, you're releasing things like serotonin and dopamine chemistry into the blood. Those chemicals promote growth and harmony. So [...] as you switch from love to fear, you change the chemistry of your blood, and the blood chemistry controls the fate of your cells. So your mind is controlling the genetics of your cells.

All feelings and behaviour are generated by Thought. How we think thought works is the biggest influence on our performance and how we experience life.

In essence

- Much of our behaviour is based on habitual or conditioned thought patterns. It isn't responsive to the moment. It's responsive to the past.

- Beliefs are not good or bad. They are just thoughts that we've sub-scribed to and we can unsubscribe to any thought at any moment.

- Thought is the ultimate performance placebo.

Chapter 6

Focus and Flow
Stay in the zone and get more time back

'There is no need to go to India or anywhere else to find peace. You will find that deep place of silence right in your room, your garden or even your bathtub.'

Elisabeth Kübler-Ross

We've become a society of multi-taskers and over-thinkers. We're distracted and busy-minded. And when we do focus on something, it's often an unhealthy or myopic level of attention. We rush from one thing to the next, always complaining that there's never enough time.

How can we experience the right kind of focus to accomplish and achieve what matters most to us?

Why a quiet mind is undervalued

Five years ago, I went to visit a mentor in the US so I could take my understanding of state of mind to a new level.

On the second day, I arrive at 10am to begin my session. After 90 minutes, I was told that it was time for us to take a pause and that I should return at 4.30pm. I had flown halfway across the world and she wanted me to leave and spend five hours on my own. To say that I was frustrated was an understatement. And my frustration definitely didn't look like it was coming from my own thinking!

As walked around the beautiful town, my agitation intensified. I called a close friend who had visited previously. I wanted to check if he had also been turfed out for five hours. He reassured me that this was 'part of the process'. I wasn't convinced.

I got more and more frustrated. I started to question whether I should even stay. What was the point? How could five hours on my own be useful compared to five hours with the person who is meant to be teaching me something. If I wanted five hours on my own, I could have done that in my home town, at no cost to me. And so it went on. Thought upon thought, my mind getting busier. I became more and more aggravated and annoyed.

I went back to my apartment where I continued to sulk.

I don't know what happened, but after about three hours my mind shut down.

I had some kind of implosion and my mind got really quiet. Unnervingly quiet. I'd never experienced that before. I thought perhaps I had bored myself into submission. I felt like I'd been lobotomised. There was nothing but pure silence. Total stillness. I spent the remaining time walking around, enjoying the unfamiliar emptiness of my mind.

When I returned to meet my mentor I shared how quiet and still I was feeling.

'Do you value this state of mind that you're in?' she asked. I reflected on her question. The stillness certainly felt nice. It also felt new and different but I couldn't honestly say that I valued it.

I realised I'd never really known what it felt like to have such a quiet mind unless it was during a yoga class and even then it wasn't like this.

I'd been living in a busy mind for so long that I thought it was normal. In fact, I believed that to get things done and to be successful, it was necessary to be constantly thinking. I was a fully paid up member of over-thinkers anonymous. I didn't place any value on a quiet mind. I also realised that I'd lived my life with a low level of anxiety humming away in the background. It had become so familiar that it felt normal. It had never occurred to me that there could be a different way to live that might be more conducive to a happy or successful life.

I used to believe the more thinking I did, the smarter I would be. Little did I know that there's an inverse relationship between quantity of thinking and quality of experience and performance.

Distinction: Normal vs Natural

Normal	Natural
What we've grown accustomed to. Something that has become familiar or comfortable.	Describes what is innate, inherent or in alignment with nature and how things work.
We acquire habits of thought or behaviour and this becomes our norm. Cultures at work are also examples of what can become 'the norm'.	
We can become used to certain feelings, certain ways of thinking, certain situations.	
We can live in an 'unhealthy normal'.	

Many of us are living in minds that are so full of noise and clutter and there are consequences for living in this mental state for any prolonged period.

Have you noticed that when your thinking slows down you remember where you left the keys? Or that when you get distracted from something you've been focusing on, you suddenly get the answer that had previously eluded you?

We live in Thought like fish live in water. We don't notice that this is the environment in which we live and breathe. And every day we have thousands of thoughts passing through our minds. In the same way that we are always breathing, we are always thinking. We live in a flowing stream of consciousness.

You've probably noticed that some thoughts just drop away. You try to hold on to a thought to share it with someone and it's gone. Some thoughts you want to get rid of but like annoying flies, they keep coming back to bug you. Other thoughts you grab on to. You feed them, entertain them and they multiply. Before you know it, your mind is so full that you can't see the wood for the trees. Your thoughts have taken up residence. They've occupied every available space.

 95% of workers say they think too much.

The question is, what's the impact of over-thinking and what can we do about it?

The overactive, busy mind is like a car that's always in gear. It's the enemy of effectiveness and productivity and the cause of procrastination and overwhelm. It clouds an otherwise clear mind and can lead to unnecessary mistakes and misunderstandings. It stops us from feeling connected to others.

EAD – Executive Attention Deficit

I walked up a familiar street in Central London and noticed a beautiful building. Despite walking up this street many times, I didn't remember seeing this building before. I must have walked past this building 100 times. I had managed to miss it every time.

Many of us spend large chunks of our day living inside our heads. We miss what is literally under our noses. It's as is if we are sleep-walking through life.

At work, we're all so busy multi-tasking. I have clients who are taking phone calls, sending emails and having conversations on a chat screen – *all at the same time*. We speak and listen to each other in sound bites.

Multi-tasking is now talked about as the enemy of effectiveness.

Publilius Syrus the Roman philosopher nailed it in 100 BC when he said: 'To do two things at once is to do neither.'

We think we can do several things at once and do them well and we can't. We're terrible at it! Our brains haven't evolved to this level. It's one thing comparing the brain to a computer but we simply don't have the multi-tasking capabilities of a brand new Apple Mac.

Professor Earl Miller, a neuroscientist at MIT, did some research that showed how doing even two tasks at once, such as making a call and typing an email, creates mental overload and slows us down.[1] Why do we do this to ourselves when common sense tells us it doesn't work?

Dr Gloria Mark is an 'interruption scientist' at the University of California. Her research reveals that as we flit back and forth between tasks, we may work faster but we produce less.[2]

Oh, and apparently women aren't biologically better at multi-tasking. According to brain research, this is a myth. The reported reason is that females tend to be happier doing more than one thing at once!

But multi-tasking isn't the real problem. It's the presence of mind that we bring to what we're doing and the impact this has on our relationships, our performance at work and our enjoyment of life.

Our minds are often so full of all the things we should or shouldn't be doing. We're suffering from EAD. It's not that we aren't paying attention. The question is, *what are we paying attention to?*

There is more appreciation now that a clear mind and clarity of thought is conducive to productivity and high performance. In recognition of this, there are thousands of books and products aimed at helping you get a quiet mind and silence that monkey chatter. We're offered different techniques and strategies, with the promise of inner peace, clarity and calm. The only downside is that many of these approaches can often add more congestion to an already busy mind.

On noticing my apparent inability to relax, a friend suggested I try meditation. She was already convinced of the benefits so I agreed to try it. Anything that promised a more serene state was appealing.

Alas, any attempts to sit still on a wooden block cross-legged and quieten my mind was at worst infuriating and at best irritating.

"If I could stop thinking, I might be able to empty my mind. Think of a blank wall... but that's still thinking... or is it?"

The more I tried not to think, the more thinking I did.

TEST IT

Try not to think of a bright pink dog or your neighbour running naked down the street.

I'm sorry if that wasn't pretty.

The very act of trying *not to think* is itself an act of thinking. Thought suppression is not the answer to a clear mind. There's a lot of research demonstrating the paradoxical effect of trying to stop certain thoughts.

A hilarious example of this is in a classic British TV series called *Fawlty Towers*. In the series, the owner, Basil Fawlty, is known for his cringe-worthy faux pas. In one episode he has some German customers in the hotel restaurant. He decides he must not mention the war under any circumstances. You can imagine what happens. He can't stop himself from mentioning the war.[3]

The more we try not to think certain thoughts, the more they want to pop right back up. It's a case of what you resist persists!

I decided that the conscious act of meditation wasn't for me. But I have to say it was a great way to see how Thought plays out in relation to focus.

People often think the goal of meditation is to empty the mind, which for many means trying to suppress or stop thoughts. This is probably why so many people struggle with meditation. I later learnt that the act of meditation is to observe thoughts as they come and go without judging or evaluating them.

This non-judgmental awareness of thought is key because it isn't our thoughts that disturb us. It's the type of attention we give them. It's how we think about our thoughts that matters.

The more we understand the fundamental nature of Thought, the more wisely we can use our minds. Thought is the greatest gift bestowed to human beings. Without it, there would be nothing.

As a solution to the over-burdened, busy-minded worker, meditation and mindfulness have become more mainstream and companies now offer yoga and meditation as part of their 'wellbeing' programmes. Whilst this may help, there's a difference between meditating and a *state of meditation*. Similarly, there's a difference between practising Mindfulness and being mindful.

Distinction: Meditating vs The state of meditation

Meditating	State of meditation
A practice.	Natural stillness and presence.

We've all experienced this natural state of stillness or peace. Some experience it when they run, when they play with their children or when they are painting or cooking. I experience it in a variety of situations including when I sing or when I'm out in nature. Any activity can be a meditative experience. You can fall into this state of mind when you're washing up or making a drink and you probably do.

If we tend to feel more peaceful in certain situations or settings, it seems logical to believe that the activity itself is the cause of our peaceful feelings. But as scientists often say, correlation isn't causation.

On many occasions, I've spent an entire 90-minute yoga class struggling to find my balance. Eagle pose becoming face plant pose and my head so busy that standing on one leg was like trying to walk on water.

Whilst it might look as if you have to do a particular activity or go to a special place to clear your mind or experience that deep feeling of wellbeing or peace, you don't. Clarity and peace of mind is your natural state.

Another way to describe this quality of mind is *being in the moment*, in *a state of flow*. Musicians and artists often talk about flow. Athletes and sportspeople describe this flow as their optimal performance state. It's often called 'the zone'.

As I've been writing this book, I've moved in and out of that flow state many times. There have been long periods of time when I've lost myself in the writing. It's as though I disappear and someone else is typing the words. It feels effortless.

Based on thousands of studies of this mental state, Mihaly Csikszentmihalyi identified several conditions which seem to exist when we are in flow.

Can you relate to any of these?

1. Total immersion and involvement with whatever you're doing.

2. A feeling of joy, an almost trance-like state.

3. An inner clarity.

4. A sense of knowing and confidence.

5. Lack of self-consciousness – i.e. operating beyond ego.

6. Timelessness – you're so in the moment, you have no sense of time.

7. Intrinsically motivated – you're into the activity for its own sake.

Flow isn't just an optimal performance state. It's also a very natural one.

When it comes to how we experience life, there are two distinct orientations: *being in* the experience vs *thinking about* the experience

Distinction: Being in the experience vs Thinking about the experience

Being in the experience	Thinking about the experience
When you are deeply absorbed in the present moment. You lose any sense of time and sense of self.	Being in the past or future. It takes us out of the present moment and out of the flow.

In his seminal work *The Wisdom of Insecurity*, published in 1954, Alan Watts says:

> 'While you are watching this present experience, are you aware of *someone* watching it? Can you find, in addition to the experience itself, an experiencer? Can you, at the same time, read *this* sentence and think about yourself reading it? You will find that, to think about yourself reading it, you must for a brief second stop reading. The first experience is reading. The second experience is the thought "I am reading".'[4]

He goes on to say: 'To understand music, you must listen to it. But so long as you are thinking, "I am listening to this music", you are not listening.'

The power of focus

Flow is the ultimate kind of focus and there's nothing we have to do to experience it. It's simply an absence of irrelevant mental congestion.

You'll notice that if you try to get into flow, it stifles it. The act of trying is what gets in our way. It's like driving with the brakes on.

People often ask 'How do I get into this flow state more often?' but a more useful question is 'How do I stay there more often?' because *you are already there*. It's your natural state.

Notice over the coming days how you innocently bring yourself out of that flow of life by where you place your attention. When the busyness of your thinking subsides, what's left is a space of stillness and calm. That silent space *between* thoughts is where peace and tranquillity reside.

A clear mind and clarity of thought is available in the blink of an eye. One thought is all that stands between worry and wellbeing, between frantic and flow and from 'meh' to motivated.

Just as the sun is always behind the clouds, clarity of mind is what exists in the absence of all the mental congestion and noise.

Focus, at its essence, is a way of describing a depth of involvement in the present moment.

My clients often tell me that distraction is a major issue in their workplace. They say that being able to stay in the moment is difficult.

According to Dr Gloria Mark's research, office workers get interrupted every three minutes on average – that's 20 times per hour. It's reported to take an average of 25 minutes to get back to the original task after being distracted.[5]

These constant interruptions impact on our enjoyment as we experience less flow and get caught up in trying to do more with less time to compensate. Naturally this affects performance.

The most fascinating thing about these findings is where these constant interruptions come from. Nearly half of these were reported as *self-induced*.

This makes total sense. Most people don't recognise that their own thinking is their biggest distraction. The gravitational pull of our incessant internal chatter feels strong and compelling sometimes.

Let's explore some classic examples of how we stifle our productivity and effectiveness by taking ourselves out of flow and how we can reverse it with just one new thought.

It's not the size of your list!

Do you ever complain that your to-do list is overwhelming or stressing you out?

It seems pretty funny when we see how illogical this is. As soon as we put Thought back into the performance formula we put ourselves back in the driver's seat of our experience.

Rachel is a client who has been learning about the nature of Thought. She shared the following story with me and I thought it was a perfect illustration of what we do to ourselves – innocently of course.

The incredible shrinking to-do list

Rachel's in bed about to snooze off. She starts thinking about all the things she needs to accomplish this week. She remembers a piece of work that isn't complete and needs to be handed in tomorrow. She starts feeling uneasy about it. She thinks of something else she needs to do and she adds it to her list. What if I can't get it done? What if John isn't there to sign off the project? Now she adds a few more things to her list. Suddenly, she's wide awake. She needs to think this through. What else has she forgotten about?

Here's what happens.

As Rachel feels more agitated, things start to seem more important and urgent. She then adds more tasks and queries to her to-do list. The list is getting longer now. As her anxiety increases, her creativity kicks in and other 'urgent' tasks pop into her mind. Suddenly she isn't just thinking about this week's work or even this month's. Her list has now expanded to include things for next month and the month after that. Her mind is now so revved up that she decides she needs a glass of milk to help her relax, so she can get to sleep. Now she's worrying about not getting enough rest for her day ahead.

As she makes her drink, she suddenly realises what's going on. She recognises how Thought has run away with itself. Instantly, all those urgent tasks just fall away. They're not important right now. They just seemed important because of the state of mind that her thinking had created.

By the time Rachel gets back upstairs, her to-do list is much shorter. In fact there is less on it now than when she first lay down. Her moment of clarity has given her a new perspective. A natural process of prioritisation has taken place.

This is the nature of Thought and the beauty of wisdom and understanding.

The myth of time

Time is a very popular conversation. Whoever invented the clock has a lot to answer for!

If you're anything like me (and 80% of the population), then you sometimes complain about time.

The third most popular reason for feeling stressed, anxious or worried at work is 'not enough time'.

It really does appear to most people that time is the issue. Well, I've got some good news and bad news.

The bad news. We've only got a limited amount of clock time in a day. It's the same for all of us – 24 hours.

The good news. We've all the got the same amount of clock time in a day!

When it comes to excelling at work, time isn't the key variable. The amount of time we have is never the problem. Why is it that a week's holiday flies by and can feel like 'no time' but waiting in a queue for 10 minutes can feel like an eternity?

The only problem we have with time is how we relate to it.

Or to simplify it further – *it's about our relationship to our thinking about time. There is no other way to have an experience of time.*

When you're at your most productive, effective or creative how would you describe your mental state during that time?

What about those days when you feel like you've been 'busy' yet you don't feel like you've accomplished anything? Are you clear and free-minded or is your mind cluttered and revved up?

One of the greatest benefits of understanding how Thought works is how it affects your clarity and focus, which in turn affects your experience of time.

Clients frequently tell me that as a result of learning about these operating principles, they now have more time in their day even though their actual workload or situation *hasn't changed.*

Sarah's story

Sarah is a senior manager working in a large organisation. When I met her, she was leading a team, managing a busy department and had a full workload.

She was feeling pretty stressed and anxious a lot of the time. She had what she described as a lot of 'frantic thinking'. She was always rushing from one meeting to the next and one conversation to the next. Her normal schedule was back-to-back meetings.

Sarah's confidence was low and while she was still highly motivated, the feelings of insecurity and anxiety were taking their toll on her wellbeing.

For Sarah, her busy schedule and the workload was a big part of the problem. She believed that if the workload reduced, she would feel less stressed and this would mean she could accomplish more, which in turn would make her feel more confident and happy.

Sarah's perspective is fairly typical: change the circumstances to improve how she operates which will make her feel better within herself.

Sarah had three major realisations when she began to learn about the inside-out nature of performance.

1. I don't need to believe my thoughts

When I met Sarah, her understanding of how life works was like 90% of people. She believed that how she was feeling and reacting to situations *was a response* to her workload, deadlines and all the other things she was dealing with at work.

As she looked towards the role of her own thinking and away from the details of her work situation, Sarah began to recognise the volume and frequency of the negative, self-defeating thoughts she was engaging with.

As with many people, she had bought into her thoughts about herself and her job, which in turn kept them alive and prolonged those negative feelings. She spent a large part of her working week living in this deflated and discouraged state of mind.

By learning about the nature of Thought, she realised that how things appeared at work was a direct reflection of how she was thinking about it – and not the other way around.

This realisation increased her understanding, and from this higher vantage point and a clearer perspective she could see that the job itself was not the problem. She had been caught up in a misunderstanding about where her experience was coming from.

2. My thoughts are my feelings

In Sarah's case they were feelings of insecurity, anxiety and self-doubt.

Because she took those feelings seriously, it reinforced the ideas she had about herself. When we engage in this kind of repetitive thinking (or any thinking) for a prolonged period of time, it can become a habit or pattern of thought. It becomes part of our story of who we are or how things are.

From this insecure and anxious state of mind, Sarah's work looked progressively more difficult. People seemed uncooperative or 'out to get her'. If someone gave her feedback or commented on her work, she took it as a personal attack. It provided more evidence that she wasn't good enough. It became a self-reinforcing loop.

As Sarah began to see that her moment-to-moment feelings were coming from her own thinking, she began to take her insecurities less seriously.

As soon as you realise that you're feeling Thought taking form and nothing else, your own wisdom has already taken over, bringing you back to clarity.

3. Busy in here = busy out there

As Sarah reflected on the role of Thought in her 'hectic schedule/busy work life', she began to see a pattern. She noticed that the busier her mind was, the busier her day seemed. The less she had on her mind, the less frantic her day was and the better she was able to deal with the workload and demands.

This insight was huge for her. It calmed her down. The *outside-in* belief that held her *frantic* thinking in place had gone.

> **When we lose a fundamental belief about how life works – an illusory paradigm – we will automatically lose all the thinking that was connected to that belief. It's a natural implication of being in alignment with how life works.**

Over the coming weeks, as Sarah's mind got quieter and calmer, her workload seemed a lot more manageable. Her ability to recognise her own thinking playing out, shaped how her day looked and felt. She was able to catch herself reacting to her own feelings and perceptions. It was as if she'd discovered that she'd been hitting herself over the head and blaming someone else for the pain it was causing.

It was a 180-degree change in perspective. This shift in consciousness is available to all of us, at any moment.

Time for a change?

In those moments when your head gets speedy or busy, notice how you're experiencing time.

When we have a revved-up mind it often seems like we don't have enough time or that time is whizzing by. In reality, it's the other way round. Your thinking creates a revved up state of mind or feeling of panic and that becomes your reality at that moment. If we take those feelings seriously, we may end up cutting corners, rushing through things or making poor decisions.

Consider this for yourself. Are there ever days when life feels overwhelming? Perhaps you have too much to do or too many demands on you. And then another day – with exactly the same workload, the same to-do list, the same competing set of priorities, you feel totally different. It all seems manageable and you feel calm and clear.

When we feel overwhelmed or rushed we can either see it as an indication of having too much to do (for example) or we can see it as an indication of over-thinking.

When we look to where we think our feelings are coming from, it will navigate us back 'home' to mental clarity.

When our minds are clear and we're in the flow of life, time may still seem to pass by quickly, but in this state of mind we're likely to be more responsive, creative, resourceful and effective.

In contrast, when our minds are full, time may still seem to move fast but to the degree that we're seeing life from the outside-in, our effectiveness and productivity will be hampered.

There is a direct correlation between our clarity of understanding and our clarity of thinking. As we recognise the inside-out nature of our experience, our minds naturally clear and we regain clarity of thought. Common sense prevails.

The lesson here for all of us is look towards the nature of Thought and away from the details of our experience. The answers are never in the experience that's already been created. It's too late by then. The answer is to look to what's doing the creating – to what is creating all thinking and feeling – to the impersonal principles of Mind, Thought and Consciousness.

Once Sarah had her own insights into how she'd been operating, things changed dramatically for her. Whilst the workload and demands of the job were the same, she began to experience them very differently. Because her thinking had slowed down and there was a lot less of it, she did quite literally get more time back.

In her own words:

> 'I'm a busy person, I've always got lots on my plate at work, there's always a number of plates spinning, but in the past I've created an existence around it that wasn't really there and by stepping away from that and realising it was thought created, means that there's time. There's time to think about strategy... time to think about coaching and team development... time that was always there but which I just didn't see before.

> 'I'm not bogged down by anxieties and worries and everyday stresses that previously would have got in the way of

me leading my team effectively. Life now is calmer, it's worry-free. I have great relationships with everybody. The relationships in my life have all got better as a result of me not having this furious thinking of my brain ticking over all the time. The change is profound'.

While your thinking may look like a reasonable response to the circumstances, that's part of the outside-in illusion. How the circumstances appear to you is a result of how you are thinking about them.

As Rory Sutherland said in his Ted talk, 'Things are not what they are; they are what we think they are'.[6]

Time is indeed one of our most precious commodities. There are only 24 hours in a day and the great news is that with a little bit of understanding about how Thought works, you can experience increased clarity, enjoy more flow, achieve better results and create more time for yourself in the process.

In the next chapter, I explore the most common achievement trap that many of us fall into, and how to escape it.

In essence

- Prioritise presence over productivity.

- Time is a resource, not an enemy or friend. How we think about it will determine how we experience it.

- Feeling overwhelmed is just a feeling created by how you are thinking about workload, time and demands.

- Focus and flow don't need to be forced. They're a deletion of what's irrelevant. Flow is a high-performance state that occurs *naturally* and contains its own source of motivation and effectiveness. It occurs as an experience of being in the present moment.

FOR REFLECTION

Over the next few days, notice the relationship between 'busy in here' and 'busy out there'.

Chapter 7

Escape the Achievement Trap

Cut the ties and fly

'Inherently, each one of us has the substance within to achieve whatever our goals and dreams define. What is missing is the knowledge and insight to utilise what we already have.'

Mark Twain

Everyone has the ability to accomplish great things and achieve spectacular results in any area of life. Human spirit and resilience has no limits. We only have to look around today to see countless examples of brilliance in every field.

Every day ordinary people achieve extraordinary things.

Paul Ridley rowed solo across the Atlantic in 88 days, racking up 3000 miles to raise money for cancer research. At 12 years old, Craig Kielburger started a charity, Free the Children, which is now a $30-million-a-year charity and the world's largest community of children helping other children.

How about the inspirational Fauja Singh, who at 100 years old was still running marathons and, more recently, Stephen Sutton, the 19 year old who raised over £3 million for charity whilst he was dying of cancer.

At the ages of 22 and 21 the inspirational Larry Page and Sergey Brin started a research project from their garage office which became Google. It revolutionised how we access data and Google is now a verb – every brand's dream.

Accomplishing great results and making a difference at work are key motivators for many people.

In my research when I asked people what makes a 'great' day at work the top two answers were:

- If I've accomplished a positive result of some kind.
- If I feel like I've made a difference.

The downside of our striving to accomplish is that we have a modern culture of over-working and over-achieving. In Japan they have the term Karoshi, meaning 'death by overwork'.

In the pursuit of getting great results and wanting to make a difference, we can get caught in the 'achievement trap'.

Here is a client's story of how she discovered this trap and how it changed things for her at work.

Jane's story

Jane is a successful leader in a large organisation. She's responsible for significant revenues and over 200 staff.

She empowers people and leads by example. As with many organisations, the sector she works in became highly competitive. The demands to deliver consistently great results against steep targets in a highly volatile market had increased.

Jane felt particularly anxious at certain key points in the working month when the demands of her work increased. She wasn't sleeping well because she was worrying so much.

She kept her anxiety at bay so that it wasn't evident to other people that she was struggling. To her team it was business as usual. However, the mental effort required to manage the anxiety was affecting Jane's clarity and wellbeing, which in turn increased her feelings of anxiety.

In her words: 'I often had a racing mind. At times I was unable to think clearly because I was worrying so much. The quality of my thinking was compromised because I was unable to keep a clear head.'

Jane knew that her thinking was a key factor but she didn't know how to change how she felt. 'My coping mechanisms aren't working anymore', she told me.

When things went well, Jane felt better but when things were particularly difficult, her anxiety would take over. In her words, 'it was a constant up and down'. She knew that she couldn't function like this on a long-term basis. She also wanted to have a better balance between work and home.

Like many of us, Jane had some invisible beliefs that she'd subscribed to without realising it. Here are some of hers, which all follow the same outside-in pattern. Can you relate to any of these?

If [the meeting/call/event goes well] then [I can feel good].

If [things don't go well] then [I can't feel good/peaceful/happy/].

If I achieve/accomplish [result] then [I can feel good/peaceful/ happy].

Other expressions of this outside-in pattern of thinking are:

- I'll be [happy/satisfied/content] when ____.

- I cannot be [happy/satisfied/content] unless _____.

- I need ____for my happiness/fulfilment/peace of mind.

- I can/could only be happy if ____.

- I'll relax when _____.

- If _____ then I can relax/feel secure/enjoy.

- I can't be happy because _____.

- I couldn't be satisfied_____.

- I need _____ to feel better about myself.

- I will feel happy/successful if/when_____.

Because Jane believed her feelings were linked to her results and achievements, this had some key implications in her day-to-day work life. And it's the same for all of us if we don't see the truth of how Thought works.

The logic of the *inside*-out paradigm is that it can only work one way.

Whenever we think it can work the other way – *outside-in* – then it's going to put a lot of extra thinking on our minds.

Whilst Jane was doing a great job, her thinking wasn't as clear as she knew it could be. Her mind was clouded by worry and anxiety. This lack of clarity made meetings feel like harder work. It was a vicious cycle. The more concerned she felt, the more it affected her level of clarity. From this frame of mind, everything seemed more challenging and complex.

If we don't understand how thought works, our concerns and worries will seem like a logical response to the situation.

In Jane's mind, her feelings of security and wellbeing were *a result* of her accomplishments and outcomes at work.

Her core belief was:

Results and accomplishments cause my feelings of security/wellbeing/happiness/upset/frustration/anxiety.

> **We live inside a cause–effect model of the world but our biggest enemy is when we think the cause is *out there*, separate to us, when in fact the cause is the principle of Thought taking form moment by moment and the effect is a feeling.**

We think the cause is some 'thing', someone, some event and we live inside of that created context.

Jane was surprised to discover that she'd been subscribing to this outside-in belief for her whole adult life. Seeing through the outside-in illusion gave her a whole new perception of work and life in general. A whole mountain of thinking dropped away.

When it was discovered that the world was round, all the 'flat world' thinking became irrelevant. It no longer made sense to think about the world in that way. That's the profound implication of understanding how things actually work.

When we see how our psychological experience works, much of what we used to think becomes instantly irrelevant because the core belief that held that thinking in place has gone.

Distinction: Attachment vs Engagement

Attachment	Engagement
When we think that our feelings of happiness, wellbeing and fulfilment are created or can be affected by our achievements or results.	When we know that our feelings of happiness, wellbeing and fulfilment are independent of our achievements and instead are the foundation for achieving great results.

In the weeks that followed, because her mind was free and clear of all the outside-in thinking she'd been doing, Jane discovered a more satisfying and fulfilling level of engagement. In her words:

> 'My quality of thinking has improved because my mind is generally calmer. I'm able to step back and be more objective, which enables me to think about the business situation and come up with ideas and be more creative and strategic. It's hard to find great solutions when the mind is full of concern or worry.
>
> 'Before learning this, it was like being on a rollercoaster where someone else is in charge, so you've got no control. Now it feels like I'm in a fast sports car and if I go too fast round a corner and get scared, I know it's me driving. I'm in control.'

If you tune into all the messages around you, you'll notice we are surrounded by the false belief that our feelings are determined by external factors. It's so entrenched in modern culture that it's easy to miss.

A recent example is an advertising campaign for the HMRC tax office. The copy said 'Find inner peace – do your tax return now'. This is probably meant to be quite tongue-in-cheek but it still makes the point loud and clear. The press release said:

I did my Tax Return early and found inner peace.

31st January is the deadline for your online Self Assessment Tax Return. If you miss it you will get a £100 penalty. So why not do it today, pay what you owe and take a load off your mind?

Self Assessment | hmrc.gov.uk   HM Revenue & Customs

> 'The campaign has been developed to touch on the emotions that HMRC found people typically experience after they have filled in their tax return, often described as a real sense of relief or peace of mind – like a weight being lifted from their shoulders. The new ads feature people from different professions experiencing this feeling of post-return well-being.'[1]

On a recent TV chat show, the guests were discussing societal problems with gambling, particularly with slot machines. They engaged in a lively debate, which focused on why slot machines are so addictive and what needs to change to reduce people's addictive behaviours.

There is no slot machine in the world that is addictive in and of itself. It's a machine. Even if it flashes brightly and calls out their name in a super-seductive tone of voice, it still isn't responsible for any addictive tendency that a person may have.

The gambler's thinking or attitude was never discussed. There was no talk of how a person's thinking contributes to their feelings of addiction.

Addiction is *first and foremost* a feeling created by Thought. It can only come from Thought. Otherwise we would all walk past a slot machine and start throwing money at it, but we don't.

When we don't know where our feelings are coming from, it can look as if life is happening *to us*. Situations can seem like they have the power to make us react in a particular way.

I remember when I first started my business, I was working on a pitch for a new consulting project. It felt like there was *so* much riding on it and the experience felt really stressful. A colleague said to me, 'You seem very attached to the outcome here'. He was right. It was if my life depended on it, which of course it didn't. My behaviours were a clear indication of how I was thinking.

Instead of letting my team get on with the job, I was micro-managing everyone, which disempowered them. I drove myself too hard and didn't give myself space to reflect and re-charge. Consequently, I felt burnt out, which reduced my capacity to be creative and responsive.

All the signs were there, just like the fuel gauge on the dashboard. The only problem was that I didn't know how to read the signs. I didn't realise what they meant.

Whether it's winning business or finding love, when people think that how they feel can be caused or influenced by results out there in the world (i.e. something other than their own thinking in the moment), the natural implication is a busy mind from all the extra thinking that this belief creates.

When we see life outside-in, it can make people feel needy and insecure which generates certain behaviours. For some it becomes about approval-seeking, resistance or avoidance. For others it becomes about controlling and dominating. Our behaviours will always make sense in the context of how we are thinking about things.

Understanding how Thought works automatically takes a whole lot off your mind. At any moment you can realise where your experience is coming from and it throws you back into the present moment.

The natural implication of seeing life from the inside-out is that all those things we think we have to control so we can feel better or do better, are no longer relevant in the light of a new understanding.

We spend less time in our heads and more time being in the moment, able to enjoy life as it unfolds.

YES BUT...

'I have to get good sales results at work. I've got rent and bills to pay for. Are you saying that's just in my thinking?'

Most of us have commitments and responsibilities in our lives. For many, work is a necessity that helps to pay rent and put food on the table.

A head full of insecure and self-conscious thinking will cloud our capacity to thrive and meet those commitments that we've signed up for. The more conscious we become of where all feelings of insecurity are coming from, the less power those feelings will have over us and the more clarity and freedom of mind we can experience.

Imagine a salesperson who believes they are only OK if they get the sale. Their behaviour is going to reflect how they are thinking. It might show up as neediness, which comes through in how they are relating to the customer. They may rush or not listen properly. When they understand where all feelings of insecurity stem from, it settles them down. They are able to be more in the moment with their customer because their mind isn't full of those outside-in concerns and worries.

Why goals don't (always) work

Goals and targets can provide a useful direction. They can help us to focus and prioritise. They can be helpful milestones that keep us on track and on purpose. For many they act as motivators. But they can also stifle our natural wisdom and motivation.

The goal itself is never the problem. The question is whether we've made our happiness or wellbeing contingent on achieving it.

Can you think of a goal you wanted to achieve or a change you wanted to make that hasn't gone your way but you felt OK anyway?

Or what about a time when you achieved something you really wanted that you thought would make you happier but it didn't?

I heard a great example of this recently. A colleague told me he'd struggled for years and made significant sacrifices to pay off his mortgage. He thought that once it was paid off he would automatically be happier. He paid it off and quickly realised that nothing had really changed and he wasn't any happier. He said 'Everything was the same but I just had more money!' He explained that he actually felt de-motivated because there seemed less need to go to work since his prime purpose was to pay off his biggest debt. Getting up in the morning became difficult and every day he would think: 'Today will be the day that I'll be happier.' But it didn't happen.

His epiphany, as he described it, was the realisation that happiness is an inside job. At that moment, he made the decision to be happy every day when he woke up. He said he has lived that way ever since.

When we make our goals or aspirations the source of our fulfilment or happiness, we innocently rob ourselves of what already exists within us right now.

If we think our good feelings come from our accomplishments or results, we can become fixated on some target or goal out there in the future. We think about tomorrow, next month, next week, and this constant preoccupation with the future takes us out of the flow of life – out of the moment. It's in the present moment that our natural clarity and wellbeing exists – in that silent space between thoughts.

Of course we need to think ahead, plan and be organised but when we innocently attach the source of our contentment, wellbeing or happiness to the achievement of the goal, we've missed the ultimate prize.

Alan Watts says about this:

> 'There is no use planning for a future which when you get to it and it becomes a present, you won't be there, you'll be living in some other future which hasn't yet arrived. And so in this way one is never able actually to inherit and enjoy the fruits of one's actions.'[2]

Here's another way to consider some key indications of an inside-out orientation and an outside-in orientation. Both of these are a moment-by-moment experience. One thought can move us in either direction.

Outside-in	Inside-out
When you believe that something other than Thought in the moment can be responsible for your feelings of accomplishment, (dis)satisfaction, fulfilment, contentment). This means that you've split Thought and feeling.	*When you know that 100% of your emotional experience is coming from 100% of Thought in the moment. Thought and feeling are inseparable. They are one.*
Your wellbeing gets attached to outcomes: 'I'm OK if this goes well/I'm not OK if it doesn't go well'.	Wellbeing is unconditional: 'I know I'm OK however this goes'.
Motivated by toxic urgency and sense of need.	Motivated by the desire to create for the sheer joy of creating and exploration.
Struggle with criticism and failure – it's personal.	Criticism and failure is an opportunity to learn and grow – it's not personal.
Never satisfied or able to enjoy achievements in the moment – always on to the next thing.	Each accomplishment, however small, is worth acknowledging and celebrating.

Outside-in	Inside-out
Your clarity or wellbeing is compromised in order to get a result: Results 1st, wellbeing 2nd.	You operate from a sense of wellbeing and clarity which supports better performance: Wellbeing 1st, results 2nd.
Survival mentality – thinking that your security or reputation is at stake.	Security is an internal experience and reputation is made up.
Action is based on 'shoulds, musts and need to' in order to resolve feelings of insecurity or lack.	Action feels like a choice rather than a 'must'.
Relationships are neglected and stifled. People can become self-absorbed and concerned with how they are doing/how they look to others.	Relationships are enhanced and deepened.
Focus is narrow or blinkered.	Focus is broader. We see, hear and notice more.
A focus on perfection and avoidance of mistakes which stifles creativity and progress.	A focus on improvement, learning and discovery which opens up the channels of creativity.
Your sense of self is hinged on your achievements – you're only as good as your results.	Your sense of self has no correlation to your achievements. You know that who you are is not your results.

The ultimate prize

Have you ever noticed how some people are never satisfied? As soon as they've accomplished something, they're onto the next thing. Each accomplishment is meant to make them feel better, happier or validated in some way.

It can seem like our unresolved needs are the cause of our dissatisfaction. But in reality, it's the other way round. It's our feelings of dissatisfaction that create the illusion of needs. It's part of the outside-in trap.

We generate needs, desires and preferences and this creates the illusion of lack. The more we think we need, the bigger the 'gap' and the less satisfied we are.

What are we striving for? What is the deeper purpose that our efforts are looking to satisfy? Many of us will spend our lives looking for fulfilment and meaning as if it's *out there* somewhere but it can only ever come from inside.

Seeing behind the curtain to how thought works means we're in on the joke. It won't make us immune from life's ups and downs. But why would we want that? Isn't the ebb and flow of life what makes it beautiful, colourful and interesting?

Happiness, (dis)satisfaction, (dis)contentment and peace of mind aren't created by the achievement of goals or results. You don't need to be more or have more to feel fulfilled or complete right now.

Satisfaction and happiness are feelings, created by how we think, which means they're instantly available as soon as we recognise what gets in the way. There's only one thought between happiness and sadness, fulfilment and frustration and between clarity and chaos.

> **'Don't aim at success. The more you aim at it and make it a target, the more you are going to miss it. For success, like happiness, cannot be pursued; it must ensue, and it only does so as the unintended side effect of one's personal dedication to a cause greater than oneself or as the by-product of one's surrender to a person other than oneself. Happiness must happen, and the same holds for success: you have to let it happen by not caring about it. I want you to listen to what your conscience commands you to do and go on to carry it out to the best of your knowledge. Then you will live to see that in the long-run-in the long-run, I say!- success will follow you precisely because you had forgotten to think about it'**
>
> **VICTOR E. FRANKL – *MAN'S SEARCH FOR MEANING*[3]**

In essence

- The belief that there's an outside-in constrains. Realisation that life is inside-out liberates.

- From an outside-in perspective, our concerns and worries will always seem like a logical response to the situation.

- The instant you realise you're caught in an outside-in illusion, it drops you back into the present moment, back to clarity.

- Goals, targets and results aren't the problem. The question is whether you've made your happiness or wellbeing contingent on achieving them.

- From the outside-in our unresolved needs will look like the cause of our dissatisfaction when it's the other way round. Thoughts of dissatisfaction create the illusion of needs and inadequacy.

FOR REFLECTION

Where have you been hinging your happiness, wellbeing or fulfilment to some goal or target out there in the future?

In relation to the goals, projects or ideas that you are currently working on, how can looking in this new direction make a positive difference for you or those you work with?

Chapter 8

Unconditional Confidence

You're always ready

'Do not go where the path may lead,
go instead where there is no path
and leave a trail.'

Ralph Waldo Emerson

There's a big industry devoted to confidence. Thousands of books and websites are focused on helping people to be more self-confident or to get their confidence back after losing it.

Self-confidence and self-belief was ranked the No.1 contributor to successfully handling difficult or challenging situations at work.

There's no doubt that feeling confident at work is important to people.

Let's compare two people who work in the same organisation. They both want to progress. They're both talented, high-potential individuals. But there is one key difference in terms of their mindset and how they operate. Jim tends to take action whether he feels ready or not. His view is that he won't know until he tries. So rather than waiting to feel confident he just goes ahead and takes the first step or two. For Jim, moving forwards isn't dependent on how confident he feels. It's not relevant.

Jake, on the other hand, tends to hold back. He's hesitant and he only wants to take action when he feels confident enough. He's waiting to feel ready. But this is a trap.

Here are some common myths in relation to confidence.

Myth No.1: Confidence comes from external sources

90% of people believe their self-confidence comes from their achievements and how well they are doing at work.

The truth is that confidence is unconditional because it's a feeling that shows up in a particular state of mind. Therefore, it isn't dependent on anything outside of your own thinking. Confidence is part of nature's design.

As children, we are naturally fearless. We ooze confidence and then we begin to learn that the world is scary or that we're not enough in some way. I used to sing for anyone who wanted to listen. Then, as I got older, I got more self-conscious and I lost that uninhibited fearlessness in relation to singing.

Things we used to do as kids without thinking, we now have a lot of thinking about!

Myth No.2: We need to feel confident before we can take action

People are often waiting for a certain feeling before they take action but the feeling of confidence isn't required.

The idea that we need to have any particular feeling before we can move forward is part of the outside-in illusion. 'I need that feeling, and then I can make that important call.'

You could find two salespeople and on paper, they could have the same amount of experience and perhaps even the same sales figures and yet one is very confident and the other isn't.

If having great skills or lots of experience in a particular area was the answer to confidence, then why do so many famous performers get just as nervous after 10 years as they did at the start of their careers? If they waited to feel confident before they performed, they would never step onto the stage.

People often shrink back from expressing themselves and stay within their perceived comfort zone because of self-doubt or insecurity.

Why would a fearful thought stop you from doing what you want or need to do?

We may think a particular thought but we don't have to listen to it. It doesn't have any inherent power over us unless we give it power.

The pursuit of confidence is over-rated and can be a distraction that gets in the way of success.

Jan is a leader in a large organisation. She was part of a leadership programme that I worked on. In a conversation with me, she said 'I want to have more presence. When I'm in a meeting, I feel like I'm invisible. I want to have my voice heard'.

Jan thought she needed more confidence. She always had lots of ideas but she stopped herself from speaking up. Her reasons for this were that her colleagues were 'loud and outspoken'. Jan didn't realise that her insecure feelings were coming from her own thoughts and had nothing to do with her colleagues.

To have more presence, we need to be more present or in the moment and the only thing that takes us out of the moment is our own thinking.

As soon as Jan became less self-conscious, she began to show up and become more visible in the room, rather than being in her head. Her impact and presence began to increase and her colleagues began to relate to her differently. The only thing that takes us out of the moment is our own thinking.

The illusion of certainty

One definition of confidence is *the state of feeling certain.*

I have worked with many people who want to have some certainty before they take action. They want to know how things are going to pan out, or have some guarantee that it'll all be OK. Can you relate to this in some way?

Certainty is another thought trap that keeps people stuck and stops them from moving forward, making them feel hesitant. This shows up in their energy and how they behave. Those at the receiving end will often sense their hesitancy and this can mean that they lose confidence in them. It can end up in a self-reinforcing loop.

So why do people crave certainty?

Uncertainty means being in the unknown and not knowing often feels unsafe or scary for people. We like to have the answers, a complete map with all the bits filled in. People often feel uncomfortable with ambiguity –

they don't like too many unknowns. As one of the leaders in my research shared:

> 'It's the fear of the unknown. You don't like something you can't see. It makes people feel insecure. Like when you were a kid. You're scared of the dark, of what's hiding under the bed; what can't be seen. Clearly people worry about 'will my job exist?', 'will my role change?', 'will I get my bonus?'

The sense of not knowing often sets us on a quest to get answers. When we get them, we feel a sense of completion. Our thinking creates a momentary high through a hit of dopamine which feels gooood. People like to feel good and will go to extraordinary lengths to avoid feeling bad. It always comes back to the feeling.

The thought of certainty gives us the illusion of security and that feels better to us. It's somehow comforting. The more we recognise our need for certainty as a desire to feel secure or safe then we can trace it back to the source. The desire for security and certainty is part of the outside-in illusion. Our misunderstanding causes us to look to the outside world for the cause or the solution.

We seek advice, opinions or approval – all in the pursuit of making ourselves feel more secure, confident, capable or ready.

As Helen Keller said: 'Security is mostly a superstition. It does not exist in nature, nor do the children of men as a whole experience it. Avoiding danger is no safer in the long run than outright exposure. Life is either a daring adventure, or nothing.'

The only kind of security that really matters is your innate sense of security and it isn't dependent on external factors. I know people who are living hand to mouth and have insecure feelings about their financial situation. I also know people who have plenty of money and also have insecurities about their financial situation.

As soon as you get even an inkling that you've taken a step to the outside-in order to resolve your feelings of insecurity, the self-correcting nature of Mind will return you home again – back to clarity. That's the beauty of this intelligent system we inhabit.

How many things have you done in your life where you started off hesitant or nervous and you now do those things without even thinking about them? If you waited to feel confident, you might never have tried.

It's the same with motivation. The idea that we need to feel motivated before we can take action is untrue. A friend of mine said recently that if he waited to feel motivated, he would never do anything!

We don't need to feel confident to take action. We just need courage. And courage means taking a leap of faith, and listening to wisdom, rather than listening to your insecurities and fears.

As Susan Jeffers' best-selling book was named – *feel the fear and do it anyway*.[1]

After all, what is fear and insecurity but a bunch of scary thoughts. Seeing through the illusion of insecure thoughts brings instant, natural confidence because it's always there. It's who we are. It's what we're made of. Only our thoughts can create the illusion that it was ever gone.

The greatest antidote to fear and insecurity is seeing its true nature. Trace it back to the source.

Another definition of confidence comes from the Latin confidentia 'to have full trust or faith'.

There is a deeper, more profound level of confidence that comes with seeing that we are always being guided and cushioned by a vast, unlimited intelligence beyond our intellect. The intelligence of Universal Mind is our ultimate safety net. It holds all the answers that our small minds cannot even begin to contemplate. Beyond the inherent limitations of our personal thinking is a vast potential from which we can live.

As people start to see life through an inside-out understanding, they often describe themselves as feeling more confident or regaining confidence they thought they had lost.

Confidence is a natural quality of a clear and free mind and the only thing that stifles it is getting temporarily caught up in the outside-in misunderstanding.

Dr Keith Blevens, clinical psychologist and single-paradigm pioneer said:

> 'Feelings of insecurity are immediately created when we innocently split thought and feeling. This is because we (falsely) believe we could be made to feel something we don't think.'

Your own realisations of the inside-out paradigm will bring natural confidence, clarity, energy and motivation to pursue those things that are most important and meaningful to you.

In essence

- You were born with natural confidence. Only your thoughts can create the illusion that it is ever gone.

- You don't need to wait for a particular feeling in order to take the next step.

- The greatest antidote to fear and insecurity is seeing where it really comes from.

Trace it back to the source.

Chapter 9

Beyond Identity
Step into your true nature

'I must be willing to give up what I am, in order to become what I will be.'

Albert Einstein

From an early age, we're taught who to be and how to be.

Until we are 1–2 years old we use our own name, for example 'John hungry' developing into 'Me hungry'. As soon as we start using pronouns, self-concept and self-image is born. Identity creation starts very young.

We get given labels. We take on other people's beliefs. We develop preferences. We learn certain values from parents and other authority figures.

I remember being told many things about my apparently 'fixed' personality traits from well-meaning teachers. I was told about my capability. And sometimes I listened. Sometimes I internalised their beliefs and made them my own.

Parental figures often want to manage expectations or guide their children but what they often do is project their own experience, their own beliefs, their own insecurities.

Several years ago I remember hearing a parent telling their child that they would never be able to do a particular type of work because they just weren't 'academic' enough. Whilst their observation of their child's learning styles and intelligence may have some merit, we can never know the pure potential that exists for any human being. The intelligent energy that we are made of and that flows through us is not something we can predict or pre-determine. But we can use thought to pre-determine and we can use thought to create illusory limitations.

There are so many examples of what is possible. Helen Keller, Roger Bannister and Nelson Mandela are shining examples of what the human spirit can achieve when we go beyond the perceived limitations of past experience. We are designed to evolve, to develop, to exceed and excel ourselves.

In his book *Dead Eye Dick*, Kurt Vonnegut writes:

> 'To the as-yet unborn, to all innocent wisps of undifferentiated nothingness: Watch out for life. I have caught life. I have come down with life. I was a wisp of undifferentiated nothingness, and then a little peephole opened quite suddenly. Light and sound poured in. Voices began to describe me and my surroundings. Nothing they

said could be appealed. They said I was a boy named Rudolph Waltz, and that was that. They said the year was 1932, and that was that. They said I was in Midland City, Ohio, and that was that.'[1]

Who we are becomes part of a story, crafted moment by moment, thought by thought. Many people live their lives through this constructed narrative.

The ultimate trap

Do you know the story of the frog and the scorpion? They meet on the bank of a stream and the scorpion asks if the frog will carry him across the stream on its back. The frog says, 'How do I know you won't sting me?' The scorpion replies 'Because if I do, I will die, so why would I want to sting you.'

The frog agrees and so they set out across the water, the scorpion upon the frog's back. Halfway across the stream, the scorpion stings the frog. As they begin to sink, knowing they will both die, the frog gasps 'But why? You promised!' The scorpion replies 'It's my nature.'

Our self-concept is a description not of who we really are but who we *think* we are. It's a collection of ideas and learned beliefs about ourselves. And like the scorpion, we can innocently buy into these thoughts as if they are real, believing that this is our true nature.

In terms of our performance, there are some important implications to having these self-concepts. For example, imagine that John, the sales manager, sees himself as a top achiever at work and he's proud of that self-image. In order to protect and validate the self-image that he's thought up, he might work himself into the ground, over promise or make poor decisions.

Whenever it looks like a person's self-concept might get threatened or violated in some way, they will often do whatever they can to protect it.

Some try to change themselves in order to be accepted by others. Instead of just being themselves, they expend enormous effort trying to manage other people's impression of them. As if we could make anyone think anything they don't want to think.

As soon as we see through the illusion – that our self-concept is Thought-created, it gives us access to see ourselves beyond our concepts.

It sets us free from the relentless effort of 'managing ourselves' or looking outside to fix something about ourselves that was never broken.

 35% of people agree that 'My self-esteem comes from me and is not determined by anything outside of me'.

65% of people disagree.

The above finding implies that the majority of people believe their self-esteem can come from somewhere other than their own thinking. Let's take the example of Joanne, who is a new manager. In her mind, recognition and praise (outside factors) increase her feelings of self-esteem, making her feel more confident and motivated.

This way of thinking may cause her to strive for recognition or to manipulate situations so that she can satisfy these feelings of self-worth. In the absence of praise or recognition, she could end up feeling de-motivated or unappreciated.

It's a classic outside-in trap. Joanne believes that her feelings of self-esteem or self-worth can come from something or somewhere other than her own thinking. But these feelings can only ever come from inside. As Eleanor Roosevelt said 'No-one can make you feel inferior without your consent'.

Self-esteem is often described as a key driver or motivator for people. In fact, psychologist Abraham Maslow, who created the influential 'Hierarchy of Needs' model, included self-esteem as part of that.[2]

He talked about two aspects of self-esteem:

1. The need for respect from others, such as appreciation, approval, acceptance, recognition.

2. The need for self-respect, self-acceptance and self-confidence.

If we believe our self-esteem is dependent on other people's appreciation, approval, acceptance and recognition, not only are we caught in the outside-in illusion (that our feelings come from something other than our own thinking), but we will work hard to ensure we get that external validation. It keeps us in a relentless cycle of insecurity and approval-seeking.

As soon as we realise that self-esteem is unconditional, a by-product of a mind that isn't cluttered with conditioned beliefs and ideas, we are free to be ourselves and do the best work we can do.

The unconditioned self

'Why are you unhappy? Because 99.9 per cent of everything you think and of everything you do is for yourself – and there isn't one.'

Wei Wu Wei

As we've explored, an attachment to a self-concept or identity can stifle our performance because there is an inclination to want to protect, defend or validate that creation of who we *think* we are. Yet when we realise that who we are isn't that story, that personality profile or that typology, we are free to simply *be* and re-invent ourselves moment to moment, thought by thought.

Protecting a self-concept is like trying to protect your shadow. The shadow doesn't really exist. It's just a play of light. And our self-concepts are nothing more than a play of thought.

Over 10 years ago I visited my friend Paul Hunting. He works with horses using them to develop authentic leaders. I spent an afternoon there to have my own experience which was magical and profound. Horses are such sensitive creatures. They have a very low tolerance for inauthenticity. They can sense it with alarming accuracy, giving you feedback in real time by how they respond to you as you work with them. As human beings we also have that natural radar but we obscure it with all our mental congestion.

During the afternoon Paul shared a powerful metaphor.

Imagine that we're all born as a beautiful diamond – *this represents who we really are*. Then we cover it up with horsesh**t. This represents our self-doubts and insecurities based on *who we think we are*. Then we cover that up with another layer of shiny varnish which represents the 'I' that we want to project to the world – *who we pretend to be in order to compensate for who we think we are*. We all have different varnishes. They might include status, material wealth or just ways of behaving. An example might be 'the joker' or the 'reliable' one or perhaps the 'shy' one. We might use other varnishes such as our family role or our job position. But our true nature is the diamond. Everything else is made up.

It's very powerful to recognise that how we relate and respond to people and situations at work is often based on our projections of *who we think we are* – our own created self-concept.

Who you   Who you think   Who you
really are   you are   pretend to be

So, here you are, playing in the movie of your life. What self-image are you trying to live up to? What aspects of your 'self' are you trying to protect?

If we had no self-concept or self-image, then any criticism, approval or judgement from others – all the stuff that people try desperately to avoid or attain – none of that would matter because there would be nothing to protect or defend.

In an unconditioned state of being, our motivation, self-esteem and self-confidence arise automatically and effortlessly. This is our natural state.

I'm not saying we need to eradicate all self-image or self-concept. This would be a pretty tall order and it would require a lot of self-monitor-ing. That's way too much thinking and effort. The problem isn't having a self-image. The problem is that we don't distinguish it as Thought. We don't relate to it as a beautiful work of fiction. We forget that we are the thinker.

Distinction: Self-esteem – our innate confidence vs Self-concept – our beliefs about ourselves

Self-esteem	Self-concept
A way of describing our innate confidence and wellbeing.	A way of describing the ideas and beliefs we have about ourselves eg. who and what we think we are.

Back in the days when I was a sales manager, they were making redundancies at one of the companies where I worked. I remember thinking what if I lost my job? What if I wasn't a sales manager? Who would I be without my job?

 46% of people agree that 'My work defines who I am'.

I had a major realisation about how much I had tied my sense of self and self-worth to my job and job title. I also recognised that a feeling of loss could also be a feeling of liberation. It was an early lesson in the power of thought and perception.

I later came to realise that the job doesn't define people – people define the job. It's only our misperception about how Thought works that leads us astray.

Our true nature is like an Etch a Sketch on which we can create anything. We can keep starting fresh in every moment.

Your story of who you think you are is not your true identity. You are not your thoughts, your past or your genetics. You are a thinker, who can think anything. And you do!

When we insightfully notice the role of thought in our experience of identity, a space opens up that allows our true self (who we are beyond all
personal constructs) to show up – an unconditioned self with innate confidence and courage.

In essence:

- Self-esteem is a by-product of a mind that isn't cluttered with conditioned beliefs and ideas.

- Self-concepts are nothing more than a play of thought.

- Who you are has nothing to do with your idea of who you are – you can
re-invent yourself moment to moment, thought by thought.

Chapter 10

Make Not Break Relationships
Work well with anyone

'A great many people think they are thinking when they are merely rearranging their prejudices.'

William James

There's no doubt that great working relationships are key if we want to thrive at work. When we spend so much of our lives with others, it's crucial that we have enjoyable and collaborative relationships. There is nothing that can't be achieved when people work well together and have a willingness to cooperate.

When it comes to how we handle difficult or challenging situations at work, 'support from others' was the second most popular answer in my research.

The second biggest cause of a 'bad day at work' was a 'negative encounter with a colleague or manager'.

'How I'm thinking about things' and 'My state of mind' were both at the bottom of the list.

As we've seen through many of the results that I've shared with you, the role of Thought is often undervalued or invisible to most of us, yet it's the key to successful relationships.

So, in this chapter I want to answer the following questions: What does your thinking have to do with relationships? And how can you leverage your understanding of Thought so you can create even stronger connections and great working partnerships?

It's not me, it's you!

A couple of years ago, I asked a group of senior account executives from a large organisation to answer some questions about conflict and relationships in advance of a training session with me. The responses were very revealing.

One of the questions was 'What are the biggest causes of breakdowns in relationships?'

They could choose between the following:

a. my own listening/attitude

b. other people's listening/attitude.

If you had to guess, what percentage do you think chose (a)?

At the start of the training, I shared the results.

8% chose (a) my own listening/attitude and 92% chose (b) other people's listening/attitude.

The group found it hilarious because we all know deep down this isn't how it works! It raised an important point about the human condition.

More often than not, when misunderstandings or conflicts occur amongst people, it's usually someone else's fault. If only *they* had listened. If only *they* communicated things more clearly. If only they understood me better.

One of the biggest breakdowns at work is not a lack of technical skill or knowledge. It's not bad processes or too much red tape. The biggest problem is breakdowns in relationship whether it's with our colleagues, bosses or clients.

When it comes to relationships, some of the most common barriers are:

- Lack of objectivity

- Defensiveness

- Dominating

- Controlling

- Insecurity

- Approval seeking

- Manipulation

- Lack of honesty

- Conflict

Whilst these might seem like separate issues, they are all symptoms or indicators of one underlying cause which, thankfully, is also the solution.

We're all using the same neutral power of Thought and creating our own separate subjective realities. So if you're watching a show or listening to a talk with 100 people, there are 100 different realities of that same show or talk being created moment by moment, thought by thought.

It's as if we are constantly putting on different pairs of glasses, each with different-coloured lenses. Every time we change the lens, the situation looks different and we respond according to our particular lens or perspective.

In the same way that you can never know if the blue you see is the same as the blue your colleague sees, no one in that room will be perceiving things in the same way as you, even when it sounds like they do. You've probably had countless examples of this where you've attended a meeting or some event. When you discuss it with colleagues afterwards it's as if you were in two different rooms because you have such diverse perspectives.

Sometimes we embrace different perspectives. We say it's healthy and helpful to have different points of view. In brainstorming for creative ideas, the diversity of opinions and ideas is encouraged.

In other contexts, we fight to have our view heard, believed or upheld, sometimes to our detriment.

The following example highlights what's possible, when we learn something fundamental about how Thought plays out in relationships.

Mary's story

Mary works in a senior role in social services. As well as having her own caseload, she also supervises other more junior social workers. As a child protection worker, she often has to deal with other agencies, schools and professionals.

In one particular case, Mary had a child who was at risk and she needed to talk with the child's Head of School to get their involvement and cooperation. She wanted to ensure that they were doing everything required to support and protect this child.

After her first meeting with the Head of School, Mary described her colleague as aggressive and uncooperative. She felt she was being personally attacked and that her competency was being questioned. As a result of this breakdown in relationship, she felt discouraged and couldn't see a way forward.

After that initial meeting, there were a few things that Mary realised when she looked in the direction of the nature of Thought.

1. Mary had become defensive but thought this was a natural response to her colleague's 'aggressive' behaviour.

She realised her defensiveness stemmed from her own expectations and ideas about how she thought the meeting should go. Her behaviour was generated from this feeling, which created unnecessary tension between them, and her colleague responded accordingly.

2. Mary saw how she had been judging her colleague based on her own feelings of insecurity. She was able to recognise that her colleague was doing the best she knew to do. This realisation brought a feeling of empathy.

Here's how the Thought-Feeling formula typically plays out in day to day interactions.

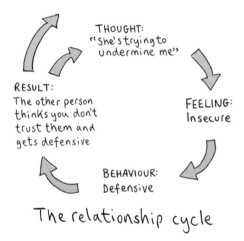

The relationship cycle

We are all operating from our own separate, subjective realities.

All relationship issues are a *paradigm problem*, not a people problem.

As Mary recognised the role of Thought in her interaction, wiser, clearer thinking replaced judgemental and defensive thinking.

3. In this clearer head space, it occurred to Mary that she didn't know what the Head of School was up against as they hadn't really made a proper connection. In that moment of clarity, Mary's heart went out to her col-

league and the next time they met they had a very different conversation. Mary's starting point was to connect with her colleague, before discussing how she could cooperate with social services.

As a result of Mary's openness to listen and understand, her colleague felt heard and it fostered a cooperative spirit between them. From this deeper feeling of connection, they began to work together to find a solution to protect their client. Not only did they resolve things but the Head of School became Mary's ally and a trusted colleague.

When we understand and recognise where our experience is coming from, common sense takes over and guides us back to clarity.

Mary didn't need special strategies or tactics to improve this relationship. All she had to do was to look in the direction of the source of her experience rather than focus on the details of the issue.

Distinction: Looking towards the role of Thought vs The details of the situation

When relationships aren't working out, which direction do you look in?

Is your attention focused on the details and content of the situation or towards the nature of the principles in your experience?

The tendency when there is conflict of some kind, is to focus on the specifics of the interactions – who said what and why, who is to blame, who should do what.

We then make further judgements and evaluations.

This is like zooming in with a camera. It expands the specific content of our thinking but reduces our overall perspective.

As soon as you look in the direction of Thought and the role that it's playing in your experience, your perspective will expand and from a higher vantage point comes wiser, more insightful thinking.

In Mary's words:

'My tendency, prior to learning about these principles, was to take people's concerns very personally and to immediately respond in a very defensive manner, taking any questions and doubts raised as a personal attack on me and my practice.

'Having an understanding of these principles has changed my experience of these situations. I now see that concerns and doubts raised are not about me as a person. The ability to see expressions of doubt and concern as Thought has allowed me to be more open to exploration with other colleagues, to be more understanding and to have more empathy with them.'

In terms of what people think most influences their state of mind, 'My relationships' is the second most popular answer.

Yet it's the other way around.

It's our understanding of state of mind that influences relationships.

As Mary's experience shows, when we are able to view things with a more neutral and objective perspective, connections improve and it's easier to work things out. Our tendency to take things personally can damage relationships. In fact, in all areas of performance, it tends to be a barrier.

YES BUT...

'Surely if I don't take things personally, it means I don't care. I want to take it personally. I want to do my best.'

We can care passionately and still remain objective, which means we're able to maintain perspective and see the bigger picture. If our primary focus is on ourselves, we are unlikely to be acting in service of anyone or anything else at that moment.

Taking things personally means that we are operating from ego. Ego is only a problem if we don't recognise it when it shows up.

If we're feeling defensive in a relationship situation, then it's an indication that ego is in the driving seat. Ego is simply a way of describing any thinking that we have about ourselves, others and life in general. It includes all our opinions, rules, judgements, evaluations and ideas of self-image.

If we think that someone or something can take away our good feelings, create negative feelings or impact our sense of self-worth, it means that we've innocently split Thought and feeling, And when we do that, it creates judgemental and defensive (ego) thinking and behaviours because we're blaming someone else for how we feel.

> 'Ego is only what you think you are and what you think of life, nothing more, nothing less.'
>
> **SYDNEY BANKS**

When we're taking things personally, it's a helpful indication that we may not be viewing the situation from clarity.

When we see or hear things with more neutrality (from the inside-out), it allows us to handle situations more effectively. Our perspective and clarity increases, changing how we respond to the other person or the situation.

Our responses, behaviours and actions are generated by *our own thinking*, not someone else's.

And that's a universal truth – it's the same for everyone. In that respect, it's never personal! We just use the impersonal power of Thought to make it personal.

Each time you get insight into the role of Thought – each time you realise that your feelings are coming from your own thinking in the moment – your understanding deepens. This helps you to consider things from a more objective vantage point – a less personal one. There is no limit to the clarity of understanding any one of us can have.

Elsie Spittle, author of *Our True Identity*, said 'Realisation is the principle of Consciousness at work'.[1] At any moment, we can realise the role of Thought in our experience. We can catch ourselves in a reaction spiral.

Your understanding of how the system works determines how you relate to and work with others. The following are implications of each orientation that also serve as indicators to wake us up to how we are seeing life.

Implications of outside-in false paradigm	Indicators of inside-out paradigm
When we leave thought out of the experience equation. When we believe our feelings can come from somewhere other than Thought in the moment. We've split Thought and feeling.	When we realise our moment-to-moment experience of reality is Thought generated. When we recognise that only our thinking can make us feel a particular way. Thought and feeling are one.
You think you need approval or agreement from others in order to validate you / your thoughts. Other people have the power to take away your sense of self-worth/contentment /OK'ness.	Other people aren't responsible for your feelings, so you don't feel reliant on them for your peace of mind or self-worth. You don't blame them for how you feel. It empowers you. It fosters more neutrality and unconditional connection.
We take things personally e.g. Getting a 'no' is a rejection of you as a person. We take criticism or feedback as a 'personal attack'. Generates self-conscious, reactive, defensive or judgmental behaviours.	You view situations more objectively with more perspective. You see that it's not about you. It's about the impersonal nature of thought and consciousness playing out uniquely in each person. Ultimately, it's never personal. It just feels personal.
We make assumptions, fill in the gaps and 'think' we know what other people think and feel.	We realise we can only ever know what we think or feel. Fosters more self-responsibility, curiosity, openness and tolerance.
People need to think like you. If they don't, it means there's something wrong with them/their judgement or there's something wrong with you/your judgement.	Everyone thinks differently. Diversity is the creative nature of Thought. Conflict is the experience of different perceptions colliding. You can appreciate difference as a natural, inevitable result of operating through our own thinking in any moment.
You feel stuck or the relationship feels stuck.	People and relationships don't get stuck. Only thinking gets stuck.
Other people have to change their thoughts or behaviour for you to feel OK. This fosters controlling, defensive or other behaviours in order to 'manage' people.	No one has to change in order for you to be OK. You can recognise behaviours as expressions of people's current thinking and state of consciousness. This fosters feelings of compassion, curiosity and understanding.

Steve's story

Steve was an unhappy manager with a very disengaged team. He was told that his management style made people feel alienated. In feedback, he was described as unapproachable, aloof and guarded. Valuable staff were leaving. He knew things had to change but he didn't know how to change them.

In his words:

> 'I was head-down and extremely serious. It felt like it was all about work. I had virtually no communication with the team. I felt very insecure and stressed, which prevented me building relationships with people and talking to my staff. I was pessimistic, rarely seeing the positives in a situation.'

As Steve learned about the principles behind state of mind, he had some major realisations which transformed his relationships and his work-life.

1. Effortless empathy

As Steve began to see life from the inside-out, it changed the way he perceived the people around him.

In his words:

> 'I've become much more understanding. I realised that they also believe they are being driven by outside factors, which gives them a lot of thinking – and that's why they say certain things, or behave in certain ways.
>
> It meant I was instantly more forgiving. Instead of looking at people superficially, I think about how they might be viewing things.'

2. The power of connection

As Steve learnt that his feelings of insecurity were coming from his own thoughts and not from the team or the job, he began to feel more confident and engaged again. He started spending time with his team.

In his words:

> 'They were so flattered that I was being attentive that they approached me much more. I started to really enjoy being with my team. I got to know them properly – their life outside work, their motivations in work. It fascinated me. I began to fall in love with them! We became a real team.'

It's all about where you are coming from

Because most of us are living from an outside-in or mixed paradigm belief system, our feelings and reactions will often seem like a reasonable response to how other people are treating us.

Our mind is more like a projector than a camera. We often don't realise that we are responding to our own perceptions.

In a conversation with psychologist Dr Mark Howard he said; 'We can only operate at the level of thinking we are at in any moment'. In this regard, we are all the same. We're all doing the best we can, based on where we think our feelings are coming from in any given moment.

By realising one simple truth about how life works, Steve experienced a complete turnaround in his work life and his personal life.

In his own words:

> 'So much has changed! The biggest change is me, and that's driven by one fact – the change in my perception of work and life generally.
>
> I no longer perceive things from the outside-in. External factors don't drive me and my thinking. *I drive them*. If there's

a difficult situation, I go back to my grounding and I realise *I'm in charge of the feelings I have about this.*

I don't become flustered. I can stay calm. It's become almost automatic.

I now see it's not about me.... I listen to others without prejudice. Instead of judging, I hear them out. And business results speak for themselves. Sales are up, market share has grown. Staff motivation is high and the team are brilliant!'

Why don't you listen?

Listening gives you access to everything you need. It connects you with your common sense and wisdom. It allows you to get out of your own way and forge deep connections with others. It's also the source of breakdowns in relationships!

As I shared with you at the start of this chapter, 92% of the executives in the programme chose 'other people's listening/attitude' as the reason for breakdowns in relationships.

Throughout my 15+ year career in sales and sales management, I thought I was a great listener until I learnt about the inside-out paradigm. It takes your listening to a whole new level.

When I am working with teams, they are always shocked at how much mental congestion they have when they're listening to others. We are so distracted by our own thoughts that it's a wonder that we hear anything.

The goal isn't to be constantly present or to remain undistracted in our conversations with others. This would be an impossible task and would end up creating more thinking as we strive to keep ourselves from being distracted!

The solution is simply to notice that you've metaphorically packed your overnight bag and left the building. As soon as you realise, it will instantly bring you back. The mind has a beautifully wise, self-regulating nature. A moment of recognition will instantly return you to the here and now.

We are always going to have thoughts flowing through our minds. But we do get to choose whether we follow them or not.

Just because we get on a train of thought, doesn't mean we have to stay on it. When you realise you're the driver, you get to choose when you stop.

How we listen to ourselves and to others and where we are listening from is a direct reflection of our own thinking in any moment.

A colleague told me a story which is a great example of how Thought affects our listening.

Whilst he saved up to get a house of his own, he moved back to live with his mum. Most evenings, he would go and visit friends. As he drove off, his mum would pop her head out of the kitchen window and shout 'Drive carefully!' He told me this irritated him. Then one evening as he was leaving his friends to drive home, one of them said 'Drive carefully!' and he thanked them. As he drove home he realised that he reacted totally differently to his friends even though they said exactly what his mum says to him.

My colleague's mum was being loving and considerate and so were his friends. Yet how he *heard* her was a function of old re-hashed thinking. We often don't realise how much mental clutter we bring into the present. Most of people's conversations are full of habitual thoughts that are well past their sell-by date. There is little space for fresh, responsive thinking when our minds are full.

How you feel about someone will always be consistent with how you are thinking about them in any given moment.

For example, if you have the thought that a client is arrogant, you are going to instantly experience that thought as a feeling. And that feeling is what you are responding to. Not them.

> ### YES BUT...
> 'My client really is abrupt and rude. Everyone agrees he is. So are you saying that it's just my thinking?'

The other person's behaviour isn't the cause of our struggle but it's often the first place we put our attention. The question is – where do you think *your* feelings are coming from? What are you blaming for your state of mind in any moment?

From an inside-out perspective – which is the only way it works – we have a thought that someone is rude or selfish and we relate to that person from the perception that we've created as if it's a reality *out there*. We instantly experience that thought as a feeling and we live in that feeling, until we have another thought.

Whenever we have an issue or a problem with someone else, it is, by definition, caused by how we are thinking about them.

In the words of Dr Keith Blevens, a pioneer of this understanding, 'It's a paradigm issue'.

The rude or abrupt client has nothing to do with our experience of them. Just like the workload has nothing to do with our internal experience of the workload.

No one and nothing has the power to determine how we experience life. Only the principles have the power to determine how we think about someone and consequently how that makes us feel. That's why we can all have different perceptions and experiences of the same annoying boss or difficult colleague.

When we get stuck in what seem like insurmountable problems and issues at work, the most helpful thing we can do is make sure we are seeing the situation with clarity and perspective. If we leave *Thought* out of the equation, the natural implication is more thinking which often leads to complexity and misunderstanding.

But... understanding how Thought works doesn't mean that all your relationships will be plain sailing. It doesn't make you immune from getting upset, frustrated or irritated with people. If only it were that easy!

Where there is a human being, there will be the potential for relationship issues. You won't always see the truth of your experience. And you will be surrounded by people who are dealing with the same human frailty. Sometimes, you'll get hung up with how other people are *making you feel*. And they will be experiencing the same misunderstanding.

But somewhere in your consciousness, your wisdom will be alive and well. At any moment, it will bring you back to clarity and with your new perspective, you'll know what to do or what not to do.

In every moment, we have the potential to start fresh. We have the potential to experience anyone with new eyes and ears – even people you have known for a long time. In fact those are the relationships where we most easily fall into the 'I know what he's going to say. I know what he's like' listening.

When we bring our memories and past experience of someone into our conversations with them, it limits how we relate to them. Rather than being responsive to the moment, we're listening from the past and from our own ideas of who we think they are – not who they really are.

We can listen and hear beyond the limitations of our own ideas and beliefs and beyond what we already think we know. We can listen from the unknown. Every moment is a new, fresh moment. Only our thinking makes it old.

In a conversation with a wonderful teacher, Robert Kausen, author of *We've Got to Stop Meeting Like This*[2], he said to me:

> **'The unknown is a bridge to deeper understanding.'**

We underestimate the power of *not knowing* and the magic that exists inside that space of possibility. When we have less on our minds, we can connect more deeply with others and create more possibility in the process.

It never really happened did it?

A client was telling me about an email that she'd been sent by a colleague. She was angry about it. I'd read the email and I couldn't see anything other than a polite request.

'He's trying to undermine me.' 'He sent it just to make me react.' 'He thinks I'm not capable of leading this project so this is his way of telling me.' She was getting more and more annoyed.

We went back over her story and I asked her again 'Is this true or did you make it up?' My client smiled as her very factual story evaporated in front of her.

'It never really happened did it?'

'No!' she shrieked with laughter.

We confuse fact with fiction. This is the sneaky nature of the human experience.

We project our thoughts outside of ourselves. We attach them to people, emails, to-do lists, traffic. What was once a little bubble of energy instantly becomes part of our reality.

When we ask 'What is fact and what is fiction in this situation?' we open the door to a whole new way of experiencing life. We begin to call into question what is real and true. This immediately creates a space for new thinking to arise.

> **Fact:** Our moment-to-moment experience of life is inside-out. It cannot work any other way.

> **Fiction:** The mistaken belief that our psychological experience can be generated by something other than the principles. The belief that there's an outside-in paradigm.

Mark Twain said: 'I've lived through some terrible things in my life, some of which actually happened.'

Yes it's true that people say things and do things that we might not like or that may be inappropriate or wholly unacceptable. But any negative feelings or emotional suffering that we might experience in relation to their behaviour can only come from our own thinking in the moment *about* their behaviour. What one person finds aggressive or irritating, another finds eccentric or sad.

No one can make you feel anything that you don't think.

When you see life from the inside-out, it won't make sense to look outside yourself to change a feeling created inside. You are instantly empowered because you're not blaming other people for how you think or feel. It liberates you.

You can also realise at any moment that they too are feeling their thoughts taking form and like you, they probably think its something or someone else causing it. We all get caught up in the same misunderstanding.

We may also choose to end certain relationships. We may choose not to spend time with certain people. Mental clarity and the wisdom it provides will guide us to make the right decisions in relationships.

It's all about the feeling

When you think about those people that you most like to spend time with, what is the feeling like between you? Do you feel connected? Are you being yourself?

When you have meetings that go really well, what is the atmosphere like?

How do you think the mood or the energy in the room impacts on the success of the meeting?

Team situations are a great way to see the nature of Thought.

I recently led a training programme with a leadership team who wanted to improve team communication and collaboration.

When we got together, and after listening to them for a while, it became clear that they had developed some entrenched habits of communicating.

Their style of dialogue was to debate everything they discussed. Debate is great if you're in a courtroom but it's not overly conducive to creating and fostering cooperation.

Distinction: Listen to confirm (reactive) vs Listen to understand (responsive)

Listen to confirm (reactive)	Listen to understand (responsive)
When we listen to confirm what we already know, we're listening from the past. We're in a **reactive** mode. We are bringing 'old thoughts' into a fresh, new conversation. Listening in this way acts as a barrier and stops us from hearing something new that may progress things in a useful direction.	When we listen to understand, we choose to park what we think we already know. We open ourselves up to be impacted by fresh and responsive thought. We step into the unknown. In this way, we are fully available and responsive to others.

When we debate, the focus is to assert our point of view. We listen to confirm what we already know, to prove ourselves right or the other person wrong.

People often pursue being right, at any cost. Being right makes us feel validated, superior or better, but it makes others wrong. Our ego will go to some lengths to avoid being wrong. The ego has no humility.

Debating is a *win/lose* mode of interaction and the antithesis of a collaborative, connecting conversation. Rather than fostering trust and opening people up, it tends to move people the other way towards a more defensive and closed way of being.

In a group setting, how do we know if we're operating from perspective and clarity? What is our guide?

When the feeling or energy drops, this is a sign to re-calibrate. But instead what you often find is that people lean in and slog away until the problem or issue is resolved. Perhaps you've experienced this with a group or team?

The feeling or energy amongst a group of people is like a temperature gauge. It's a crucial guide that lets us know whether we have enough collective clarity to continue. Remember that our thinking will always trick us into believing that it's valid and credible.

So whenever this particular leadership team noticed that the energy had changed – that perhaps people were withdrawing, getting defensive or becoming frustrated, intense or disengaged – it was a sign for them to pause, re-connect and re-calibrate.

If you want your meetings, sessions or conversations to go well, put state of mind first. It's the most valuable thing you can do.

Is love the answer?

Could love be the secret ingredient for successful relationships at work? Could it be the key to more motivation or better performance? Or is this just a touchy-feely thing that should be reserved purely for hospitals and care homes?

Harvard did some research called 'What's Love Got to Do With It? The Influence of a Culture of Companionate Love in the Long-term Care Setting'.[3] They wanted to find how a work culture that was focused on compassion and love would impact on people's performance.

They started with people in a health-care setting and then rolled it out across different industries from financial services through to real estate. They saw consistent themes.

What they discovered is that where there's a culture of love and compassion, people do better. There is a direct link between the amount of warmth, connection and care that people feel at work and how engaged they are.

They saw positive changes in wellbeing and accountability. In this kind of culture, the relationship and the feeling amongst people is the priority.

In an article describing the research, the authors, Sigal Barsade and Olivia (Mandy) O'Neill, said:

> 'You might think all this love business would be hard for some people. We did, too, before we started this study, but we found love in some unlikely places. For example, we talked with employees at a large aerospace defence contractor who told us about a newly acquired division that had a strong culture of love.'[4]

The results of this research shouldn't really be a surprise to anyone. Love and happiness seem to be the two things that people desire more than anything else. It seems that everything we do is in service of feeling happy or feeling love.

Recently, a client was telling me about a challenging relationship with a colleague. 'Do I really need to like them to work well with them?' he asked.

There was a time when I might have said no. but when we have an appreciation for the importance of that feeling of human connection, then the answer has to be yes.

But there is something else here too. What is this business of likes and dislikes that we humans have?

What if all likes and dislikes – *all preferences* – were just thoughts that you have bought into over time? What if you related to them as thought habits, rather than relating to them as truths. After all, they are made up.

I'm not saying we should ditch all our likes and dislikes, but there is way more freedom in our experience of life when we see our preferences for what they really are – *Thought*.

When preferences become part of people's fixed reality – i.e. 'this is how it is' – then it can limit possibilities in all areas of our lives. With less attachment to your preferences (your thoughts) you may find that connecting with others is much easier.

When it comes to deepening connections at work, most books and training programmes will give you a bunch of things *to do* in order to get rapport and build relationships. This reveals a major myth about rapport and connection.

Relationship Myth: Rapport is a process. It's something we have to manufacture.

Distinction: Rapport as a process vs Rapport as a natural connection

Go to any busy restaurant and you will see people in deep states of rapport. You'll see certain behaviours such as mirroring of gestures. But this isn't a conscious act. It happens naturally.

However, this naturally occurring experience has been turned into a set of techniques so that we can try to engineer rapport. For example, we can mirror and match people's words, gestures and other behaviours. The problem with this approach is that people know intuitively when the connection isn't genuine and when someone is consciously trying to manufacture one.

There is nothing we have to do to get rapport. Rapport and connection happen naturally when our minds are free of self-consciousness, concern and insecurity.

Lack of connection is the innocent misuse of Thought. Love and connection is the natural implication of a free and clear mind.

Connection with others is part of nature's design. We *are* already connected. And this is more than just a philosophical issue. From a scientific perspective, we are all pure consciousness, pure energy interacting with each other. We're all made of the same stuff.

The idea that we are separate is just the way we use the power of Thought to create an illusory separation. Whilst I am here and you are there, at an *energetic* level (the most influential level), we are connected. And we all use the power of Thought to create our own little worlds, our own personal realities.

In her fascinating book, brain scientist, Jill Bolte Taylor, describes her experience of having a stroke and what happened to her mind in the process. She says:

> 'My entire self-concept shifted as I no longer perceived myself as a single, a solid, an entity with boundaries that separated me from the entities around me. I understood that at the most elementary level, I am a fluid. Of course, I am a fluid! Everything around us, about us, among us, within us, and between us is made up of atoms and molecules vibrating in space.
>
> 'Although the ego centre of our language centre prefers defining our *self* as individual and solid, most of us are aware that we are made of trillions of cells, gallons of water, and ultimately everything about us exists in a constant and dynamic state of activity. My left hemisphere had been trained to perceive myself as a solid, separate from others. Now, released from that restrictive circuitry, my right hemisphere relished in its attachment to the eternal flow. I was no longer isolated and alone. My soul was as big as the universe and frolicked with glee in a boundless sea.'[5]

This may seem like an esoteric thing to share in a chapter about relationships but until we see something deeper and more fundamental about the nature of being human, we will continue to get caught up in the endless thought traps that our thinking creates.

Love is the fuel of relationships and it's always there – it's our natural state. The only thing that stops us feeling a deep level of connection with others is our own self-conscious, judgemental or insecure thinking, stemming from the mistaken belief that our feelings can come from somewhere other than our own thinking.

In essence

- Many of the relationship problems we experience at work are a paradigm issue, not a people issue. They are symptoms of a misunderstanding about how Thought works.

- We all live in separate created realities – *my blue will never be your blue* – and yet we are all connected via one universal state of consciousness.

- Love and compassion are the fuel of relationships.

- Lack of connection is the innocent misuse of thought. Love and connection is the natural implication of a free and clear mind.

Chapter 11

Decisions Made Easy
Navigate by wisdom

'The intuitive mind is a sacred gift and the rational mind its faithful servant. We have created a society that honours the servant and has forgotten this gift.'

Albert Einstein

For most of us, making decisions and choices is an important part of our lives. Depending on the type of work you do, there may be varying levels of risk in the decisions you have to make.

For example, in the case of a child protection social worker, the lives of children may be at risk so the assessments and decisions a social worker makes are critical, as is the level of clarity from which they make them.

For doctors or surgeons a split-second decision could affect someone's long-term health. Then, perhaps at the less risky end of the spectrum, workers in all fields are making choices about which strategy to go with, which person to recruit for their new team or which headline to choose for tomorrow's paper.

Many of the decisions we make are complex and the time we have to make them can vary greatly. But it's not just the complex decisions that prove challenging to people. Sometimes we can make the simplest decisions very complicated!

What makes decision-making difficult and how can understanding the nature of Thought help us to make better decisions?

What gets in the way of good decision-making?

> 65% of people say they have made decisions at work that they've later regretted.

Sometimes we just get it wrong. We make decisions that we later come to regret. That's life and we can't always expect to get it right.

When I asked people the top reasons for making regrettable decisions, here's what they said:

> The top five reasons for making regrettable decisions at work are:
> 1. Too much haste
> 2. Having incomplete or incorrect information
> 3. Being overwhelmed
> 4. Lack of clarity
> 5. Feeling insecure

As we've explored in previous chapters, most people will think that too much haste, lack of clarity, being overwhelmed or feeling insecure are caused by the situation.

In reality, they are all symptoms or implications of *one* thing.

Let's take a look at some of these through the lens of the principles behind state of mind.

Too much haste

Why do we rush into making decisions? Perhaps someone senior – a boss or client for example – is pushing us because of their own time constraints. But quite often it's our own lack of clarity or insecure thinking that leads us to act too quickly or to avoid pushing back or asking the important questions.

Being overwhelmed

Whenever we feel a sense of being overwhelmed, it's a signal that we're over-thinking. The feeling of being overwhelmed can only ever come from how we're thinking about the decision we're making. Whilst it might look and feel like it's related to something else, it only works one way – inside-out.

Feeling insecure

We can come up with lots of justifications for our insecurities. We may say it's because we need to get the decision right. Perhaps we want to avoid making a bad decision. We might think there's a lot riding on it which makes us feel a sense of pressure. We may have people relying on us for our decisions and don't want to let people down. But as we've explored in some depth, any feelings of pressure or insecurity can only come from how we're thinking about the decision and not from anywhere else.

Feelings of insecurity are an indicator that you're seeing life from the outside-in – that you've momentarily split Thought and feeling. Put them back together and you'll see with new eyes and hear with renewed clarity.

Lack of clarity

Sometimes we are reliant on others to provide us with vital information or support which helps to bring more clarity to the decision-making process. Often our own lack of clarity is a function of over-thinking, as mentioned above.

Most people seem to agree that having a clear head is important when it comes to making decisions.

87% of people say they put off making decisions when they know their head isn't in the right place.

This finding assumes that we know when our head isn't in the right place, but the outside-in illusion can be *very* elusive. We are brilliant at convincing ourselves and justifying our thinking. We can often believe that we're seeing things with perspective.

Good decision-making is a game of deletion. How much of your thinking is relevant right now to the decision you are making? How much of your thinking is outside-in? Mental clarity is the absence of irrelevant thought. That's why we need an internal compass. We need a reliable way to check if we're seeing life through the right paradigm – the only paradigm.

Listen to your instincts

A common assumption about decision making is that gut feeling is not a reliable source for making important decisions.

An interesting study by Mikels et al. (2011)[1] cited by Jeremy Dean on his excellent site Psyblog[2], describes how using our gut feeling for quick decisions leads to better outcomes. In one of the studies he says 'the number of participants getting the right answer went up from only 26% in the detail-focused condition to 68% in the feeling-focused condition'.

The study points to how our feelings are the most reliable indicator in these time-limited situations. You might call it gut instinct, sixth sense or intuition. We've all had those times when *we just know* what the right thing is to do. My research supports this.

> **82% of people sometimes make decisions purely on instinct or gut feeling.**

There's growing evidence that most of our daily decisions are not rational, logical thought processes but are inner-directed via instinct, intuition, gut feeling.

> **77% of people say there have been times when they've had an instinct or gut feeling about a decision at work but they ignored it.**
>
> **Of those people, 70% said their instincts were later proven to be correct.**

These results highlight something very important.

We often know what the right answer is or we at least have a strong sense of the right direction and yet many of us ignore our hunches, which in many cases turn out to be valid.

If our instincts or gut feelings are such a valuable guide for navigating the complexities of work life, how can we learn to more confidently trust our wisdom and better judgement? What's the key to that and how can it help us to make better choices and decisions at work and in life?

The top two reasons people give for ignoring their instincts at work are:
- Lack of power to make the decision.
- Lack of confidence in going with their instincts.

What role does our thinking play in these reasons?

Lack of power

Whilst you may not have the ultimate responsibility to make certain decisions, you probably have a lot more influence or leverage than you give yourself credit for. The difficulty with instinct is that it doesn't tend to have much of an explanation to go with it. By its very nature, it's fairly data light because it's a hunch, a feeling, a sense... and for those in the 'firing line' this often doesn't feel robust enough.

A senior leader told me recently that she had a strong hunch about a decision they needed to make but when she shared it with her boss she was told that he couldn't sell it through based on a hunch. Her hunch turned out to be right and would have saved them a lot of time and money.

If you have a strong feeling about a particular direction, it's helpful to remember that the person you need to influence may also be feeling insecure about getting the decision wrong. The job is therefore not to convince them that you're right but to help them see past the limitations of their own thinking. They will have had their own experiences of using their instincts, so that's the place to connect with them.

Lack of confidence

One of the biggest barriers to making good decisions is insecurity, as we've already explored. People get filled with self-doubt and hesitancy and if they listen to these feelings, it obscures their wisdom and common sense.

One of my clients had a first-hand experience of this. Sophie didn't feel she could trust her own judgement so she was asking a lot of people for their input and advice. The reality was that she knew what she needed to do but she had bought into her own insecure thinking. Rather than seeing it for what it was, it looked real and true to her. The more she looked outside for validation and input, the more clouded and confused her thinking got.

One day she got an insight about how Thought was playing out.

In her words:

> 'All I have to do is open my eyes, take a deep breath and remember that it's not about what's going on out there. It's just about what's going on in my head at the time... just thinking about me for a few seconds, calming down and suddenly everything else just falls away – all the anxiety, all the deadlines, all the pressures, the voices of everyone else just disappear and all I'm left with is a clear head, where I can suddenly start to hear my own voice again and then I can start to make those decisions.'

Wisdom is part of who you are – it's part of nature's design. We all have access to an unlimited source of intelligence that goes far beyond our intellectual knowledge base.

> 'The intellect has little to do on the road to discovery. There comes a leap in consciousness, call it Intuition or what you will, the solution comes to you and you don't know how or why.'
>
> ALBERT EINSTEIN

We can't always call it right, and sometimes there is no right decision but as you'll see in the next section, there are things we can factor in so that making decisions becomes easier and we can increase our chances of making the right choices.

Your thinking is often biased

There are going to be some habits of Thought that have become part of your world view. In psychology they're known as unconscious bias and we create them to help navigate all the choices and decisions we have to make every day. But they can also act as constraints in our thinking and because they tend to be in the background of our minds, they are often shaping our decisions without us realising it.

So how is it useful to know this?

Recognising that these beliefs or biases exist gives us more immunity from them. Rather than being a victim of our habitual thought patterns, we can choose to make more conscious and responsive decisions. We can choose to step back and check whether we are operating from wisdom (fresh responsive thought) or habit (old, reactive thought).

Some common biases are:

CONFIRMATION BIAS

Do you like it when people agree with you? Go on, admit it. You love being right!

Human beings have a tendency to seek agreement and approval. It gives us a sense of validation. This hidden thought trap can cause us to seek out perspectives and ideas that validate our own. At the extreme, it causes people to ignore or dismiss important insights or data because it somehow threatens their self-concept or opinions. These are all indications of outside-in thinking.

POST-PURCHASE JUSTIFICATION

There was some Harvard research done back in the 1990s which said that we buy based on emotion and then we justify it afterwards with our rational or logical thinking.

This bias shows up when we make a purchase that we later regret. Rather than be honest, we justify our decision to make ourselves feel better or more validated in the eyes of others. Again this is a great indicator that we've forgotten where our feelings come from. It's based on the outside-in belief that other people's opinions of our actions can make us feel a particular way. Only *our thinking* about their opinions can make us feel anything.

BANDWAGON BIAS

People often get swept along with the crowd. We can get into a 'group think' mentality. Sometimes this behaviour is driven by a fear of standing out or being criticised. It's based on the false idea that our feelings of self-worth, security or OKness are defined or created by something outside of our own thinking.

While there is wisdom in the crowd, you are connected to an unlimited source of wisdom that's always guiding you.

Don't confuse past experience with common sense

It often feels familiar and safer to base our choices and decisions on what's worked in the past – whether that's yesterday, last year or 10 years ago. Whilst valid in some situations, it might be driven by insecurity rather than guided by wisdom. So how do you know the difference?

Wisdom is fresh thought. It's not based on the past. It's responsive *in the moment*.

Wisdom has no rules, therefore it doesn't subscribe to what's gone before. That's why we sometimes get stumped or insecure when our wisdom offers up an idea or solution. We can get into thinking 'Can I really do this? What will people say? What if it doesn't work?'

Wisdom has a different quality of feeling to our old, conditioned and more familiar ways of thinking.

We succumb to the familiar, to what people call their comfort zone, but as Seth Godin says in *The Icarus Deception*, 'We assume that what makes us comfortable also makes us safe'.[3] The reality is that what we call the safety zone isn't really safe, it's just familiar and we confuse these two things. What we call our comfort zone is just an expression of our ease in a particular context. For example, you've been doing the same job for a few years and you think 'you can do it standing on your head'. It's familiar and so you think of it as safe.

Seth Godin also describes art as 'a leap into the void'.

The void is the unknown. It's a sea of pure potential and it is only our attempts to cling on to the familiar that keep our minds busy and stops us from discovering that infinite potential.

Good feelings don't equal wise decisions

When people are learning about these principles, they sometimes assume that if their thinking is positive and optimistic then this means that it's trustworthy or credible. A good mood doesn't equal reliable thinking. In reality, our good moods can be just as delusional as our low moods!

As human beings we are brilliant at justifying our thoughts and feelings. We might be very pleased with ourselves – in a 'positive' feeling – and yet it could be based on outside-in thinking. For example, we apologise to someone to make ourselves feel better or more superior. In this case, our actions are not coming from clarity.

Our emotions will always influence our decisions in some way, so it's important to make sure we use them wisely. The ultimate guide in any given moment is to notice... where do you think your feelings are coming from?

True emotional intelligence comes from understanding the nature of our experience so that we can be more responsive and less reactive.

Common sense and wisdom don't always come in a shiny positive package.

There is a difference between feeling happy and having clarity. There have probably been many times when you've had absolute clarity and perspective but you haven't necessarily felt happy. You may even have felt sad.

When you have that instinct or that knowing, it isn't about positive or negative. It's just about listening to that deeper feeling or voice that's guiding you.

> **'Common sense isn't common to the ego, it's before the ego... it's a deeper dimension of wisdom that we all have access to.'**
> SYDNEY BANKS

Your own wisdom and clarity is your best guide when it comes to making decisions or setting a direction. It's your North Star and it's always pointing you towards the best course of action. All you have to do is listen.

In essence

- Our biggest barrier to great decision-making is over-thinking.

- Feeling overwhelmed, unclear and insecure are all indications of outside-in thinking.

- You can mitigate against unconscious bias by becoming more conscious of the thinking that shapes your decisions in any given moment.

- Good feelings don't always equal wise decisions.

- Wisdom is our greatest guide for making decisions. It has no rules. It's neutral and responsive and comes from the pure intelligence of Mind.

Chapter 12

Keep Bouncing Back

Be a better surfer

'You are the sky.
Everything else – it's just the
weather.'

Pema Chodron

The ability to bounce back quickly after setbacks is a key attribute of high performers. We all have the ability to be discouragement-proof *regardless* of the challenges we are dealing with.

The road of life has bumps and dips and unexpected sharp corners. Sometimes it's well lit and other times it's hard to see.

We will have our challenges and triumphs. Many of us will have moments when, even if just for a moment, we doubt whether we can handle what life has dealt. Our best-laid plans will crumble in our hands. We'll get disappointed sometimes. Life will seem unfair or unjust.

Sometimes we will compare ourselves to others. We may have moments of guilt. We might think we're unworthy or not enough. We may think we're superior and somehow more deserving than others. All of this is part of our creating. It's a sign that tells us we've taken a wrong turn. It's a temporary lack of clarity.

Resilience is your innate ability to return home to your *natural state*.

Mental health or mental clarity are simply ways of describing our natural or 'default' state. You know when you are there because your mind is clear and you feel connected to life. You're in the moment, in the flow. Everything is as it's meant to be.

We don't have to learn to be resilient. We already are resilient, beyond measure. Our ability to excel, to go beyond what we think is possible, is a result of transcending conditioned ways of thinking – of understanding the inside-out nature of life.

Life is a journey of deletion, not addition. It's a lessening, a reducing of the clutter and noise that contaminates an otherwise clear, loving and wise mind.

As we make the journey through life, we have two invisible friends that travel with us. One is called Memory and the other is called Imagination. Memory tends to focus on the past and Imagination is more interested in the future. They both add huge value to our lives and, like many friends, they like to help us out from time to time.

Memory reminds us about important things. It helps us learn and grow. Imagination takes us on amazing adventures into the future, creating endless new possibilities. But Memory can sometimes get confused and because Imagination is so clever, it often gives Memory a helping hand.

It can be hard to know who's in charge. And there are times when they act more like enemies than friends. Memory will try and overpower Imagination, keeping us locked in the past, stopping us from moving on. And Imagination will try and freak us out by creating scary scenarios that we believe are real.

Fortunately they're both made of Thought. They just happen to play different roles in the drama called 'my life'. And because they are made of Thought and because you have common sense and free will, you can engage with them in any way you want.

If Memory invites you out, you don't have to go along. And if you do, you can choose to keep some distance. If Imagination starts taking you to places you don't like, you can part company.

Love and fear

We are emotional beings. We feel and this is what makes us human. People will go to extraordinary lengths to feel good and to avoid feeling bad.

All the emotions that we experience can be boiled down to two primary orientations. Love and fear. Whilst we have an evolutionary response to fear (as explored in Chapter 4), the majority of fear we experience is not in response to genuine, life-threatening danger. It's insecurity – a response to a misunderstanding about our psychological experience.

Does it make sense that a person whose mind is clear and unburdened will be experiencing feelings of anger, bitterness and jealousy? Or will they be feeling love, gratitude and connection?

All negative feelings are fear based. We may give them different names but they arise from fear.

Insecurity, anxiety and jealousy are expressions of fear.

Gratitude, joy and optimism are expressions of love.

In any single moment, we are either operating from love- or fear-based thinking.

In an interview with Oprah Winfrey, Marianne Williamson said: 'The relationship of love to fear is the same as the relationship of light to dark. Darkness is not a thing. It's the absence of a thing. So if you want to get rid of darkness, you can't hit it with a baseball bat. You turn on the light and the darkness disappears.'

When we are in a loving feeling, fear cannot co-exist in that feeling. Light removes darkness. Love is what is always behind any fearful or insecure thinking.

The beauty of understanding the principles behind our state of mind is that we don't have to practise cultivating gratitude or love. These feelings arise naturally when we notice – in the moment – where our experience is coming from.

We don't have to avoid negative feelings or strive for positive ones. It's that resistance and striving that reduces our clarity and wellbeing and gets in the way of the natural ebb and flow.

The mind is self-regulating. It's naturally wise and healthy.

Our worst enemy is our innocent misuse of Thought and our propensity to lose sight of where our experience originates.

But... we are all in the human condition.

Despite having some understanding of these principles, turbulence on aeroplanes was firmly in my list of *experiences that have nothing to do with Thought*. It wasn't until that day en route to Tokyo that I realised just how many other situations also don't look like Thought. They look real and true.

However insightfully you see the nature of these principles, there will be times when Thought will be utterly invisible to you. As my friend Gabriela once said to me, 'It's like a game of peek-a-boo. Now you see it, now you don't'.

At home we call this the 4th principle. It refers to any situation or experience that we believe is the exception, i.e. the principles of Mind, Thought and Consciousness do not apply. For example, if I fall out with my sister, my thinking has nothing to do with my upset or annoyance. It's totally down to her.

After the earthquake and Tsunami in Japan in March 2011, I travelled to Osoka to teach. Once again, I found a 4th principle – an example of a situation that must surely be the exception to the 'inside-out rule'. As the training commenced, I was faced with people who had lost loved ones or knew people who had been displaced. Some had spent time in affected areas, providing support to those most in need. It was hard for them to see the role of Thought as having any relevance in their suffering. I felt compelled to agree with them. I had to stop and question the validity of these principles and of this single paradigm that I was devoting my life to teaching.

As we sat and reflected together, we began to see a deeper truth. Yes the Tsunami was devastating. It had displaced thousands of people with a confirmed death toll (as of February 2014) of 15,884. But as the conversation unfolded, participants shared stories of resilience, bravery and hope and they also became conscious of the variety of different ways that people were responding to this event. Some of those most affected were feeling grateful and hopeful while others in the same family or the same village were struggling to get through the day.

The beauty of looking to the inside-out nature of life is that we can keep learning and enjoy the benefits that insight brings.

The ultimate thought trap

Fleas have the amazing ability to jump over 100 times their own height.

If you put them in a jar with the lid on, they will naturally jump up and try to escape. Over and over they will try. After a while of banging their heads, they adjust their perspective and jump only as high as the lid. When the lid is later removed, the fleas continue to jump but only as high as the lid. They remain trapped in the jar because they don't notice that there is no lid.

For us, Thought is the lid on our understanding of how the human operating system works. When we go beyond the limitations of our conditioning, we fall into a realm of deeper feeling, pure potential and infinite possibility.

We've all had those moments where we feel totally connected with life. Totally in the flow. We have a moment of divine inspiration. It lights us up. Then we begin to think... we start to question, to doubt. One thought feeding on the next. And we ride rough-shod over our inspiration. We stamp it out. We tell ourselves it was a crazy idea. It won't work. What was I thinking... Who am I to...?

We stack reason upon reason. It becomes more compelling. The flame of possibility extinguished in a matter of moments.

And then we see it. We catch ourselves in the act of our own undoing. And we're back again. Back to clarity – back to possibility and once again we feel hopeful and inspired. All of this in under 60 seconds.

Life isn't about controlling the waves as they come and go. But we can learn to be a better surfer and ride the waves with more grace and ease.

Our ability to bounce back is our true nature. Dr Roger Mills, a pioneer of the inside-out paradigm, said of resilience 'It is so natural in fact, that often we only notice it in its absence'.[1]

We're designed to thrive and evolve. It's inevitable if we allow it.

Every moment is a brand new moment. One thought can move us from hell into heaven and from chaos to clarity.

The ultimate influence on your sense of fulfilment, connection, motivation and your ability to flourish is *how you think life works*.

Every day we can continue to insightfully discover the pure potential that exists, unfolding with each new thought.

You are the sky.

Summary of Terms Used

The following are broad definitions for the terms used in the context of this book. In some cases, they may differ from traditional definitions or from those you are more familiar with.

COMMON SENSE: an insightful and objective level of clarity that occurs spontaneously and guides us in a healthy direction.

CONDITIONING: the process of learning that starts from birth and continues throughout our lives. It is fundamental to our ability to navigate through a physical world. We learn to open doors, dress ourselves, walk and talk. These are useful and necessary types of conditioning.

Other conditioning includes the collection of ideas, beliefs and assumptions about ourselves and the world, some of which may limit our potential and create unnecessary barriers.

CONSCIOUSNESS: is pure awareness – neutral and universal. We are pure consciousness. When our consciousness is combined with Thought it generates our personal or subjective experience of reality.

EGO: self-image, self-concept. It is the 'I' or 'me' that our thinking creates. It includes everything we think about ourselves and the world. It includes all our beliefs and judgements. It is part of our created story of who we are, including our personality.

INSIGHT: realisation via fresh or new thought that deepens or simplifies our understanding. Insights occur spontaneously from the intelligence of

Mind. Insights cannot be summoned at will. As they occur, they update our existing understanding bringing increased clarity.

MIND: the formless and universal intelligence behind life. The ultimate power source that allows us to experience the mystery of life using the principles of Thought and Consciousness.

MINDSET: attitude, outlook, perspective. A way of thinking or feeling about something. It can encompass certain beliefs which have given us a particular attitude towards something. In that way, mindset is often conditioned rather than spontaneous and responsive to the moment.

MOTIVATION: the desire, will or energy to engage in life in a particular way. It isn't dependent on anything outside of you. It arises from the pre-existing intelligence of Mind.

SELF-CONCEPT: a collection of ideas of who we think we are.

This includes self-image: how we think about and perceive ourselves as individuals. Our self-concept is part of our individual thought systems and an aspect of our conditioning. We acquire our self-concept through childhood, into adult life. It is an expression of ego thinking. It's not to be confused with our true nature, which is *beyond and before* thought-created concepts.

STATE OF MIND: a temporary mental state generated by how we are thinking and feeling in any moment.

THOUGHT: the formless creative potential for human beings to create any thought content and experience it as their reality.

THOUGHT SYSTEM: a collection of learned ways of thinking. A belief system that is personal and individualised. Also described as conditioning and habits of thinking.

Distinctions Used Throughout the Book

These are just metaphors but I hope they're useful.

What did you think of this book?

We're really keen to hear from you about this book, so that we can make our publishing even better.

Please log on to the following website and leave us your feedback.

It will only take a few minutes and your thoughts are invaluable to us.

www.pearsoned.co.uk/bookfeedback

Notes and References

Introduction

1) Miller, D. (2001). Successful change leaders: What makes them? What do they do that's different? *Journal of Change Management*, 2 (4), pp.359–368. [online] Available at: <http://www.tandfonline.com/doi/pdf/10.1080/714042515#.VCPUP_ldXOE>

2) Keller, S. and Aiken, C., McKinsey & Company report (2008). The inconvenient truth about change management. [online] Available at: <http://www.mckinsey.com/app_media/reports/financial_services/the_inconvenient_truth_about_change_management.pdf>

3) Campbell, M. and Simmons, J. (2014). At Davos, rising stress spurs Goldie Hawn meditation talk. [online] Available at: <http://www.bloomberg.com/news/2014-01-20/at-davos-rising-stress-spurs-goldie-hawn-meditation-talk.html>

4) Three Principles Movies [online] Available at: <www.threeprinciples-movies.com/index.cfm/resources/books/>. See also: <www.chantal-burns.com/research>

Chapter 1

1) Pink, D.H. (2010). *Drive: the surprising truth about what motivates us.* Edinburgh: Canongate Books, p.44.

Chapter 2

1) Sutherland, R. Perspective is everything. [online] Available at: <http://www.ted.com/talks/rory_sutherland_perspective_is_everything?language=en>

2) <http://www.threeprinciplesmovies.com/index.cfm/research/>

3) Banks, S. (1998). *The missing link: reflections on philosophy and spirit.* Edmonton, Canada: Lone Pine Publishing, p.21.

4) Ibid., p.32.

5) Ibid.

6) Ibid., p.49.

7) Pransky, G. (2001). *The relationship handbook: a simple guide to satisfying relationships.* La Conner, WA, USA: Pransky and Associates.

8) Banks, S. (1998), p.39.

9) Pransky, G. (2001). *The relationship handbook: a simple guide to satisfying relationships.* La Conner, WA, USA: Pransky and Associates.

10) From author's personal conversation with Keith Blevens and Valda Monroe.

Chapter 3

1) James, W. (1892). *Psychology: the briefer course.* New York, NY: Henry Holt and Company, p.335.

2) James, W. (1890). *The principles of psychology, Vol. 1.* [Not sure of original publisher.]

3) Blevens, K. and Monroe, V. BlevensMonroe: home of the 3 principles paradigm. [online] Available at: <http://blevensmonroe.wordpress.com/>

Chapter 4

1) Wilson, A. (2013). Jonathan Trott leaves England's Ashes tour with stress-related illness. *Guardian* [online]. Available at: <http://www.

theguardian.com/sport/2013/nov/25/jonathan-trott-leaves-england-ashes-tour>

2) Health and Safety Executive (2014). Stress-related and psychological disorders in Great Britain 2014 [online]. Available at: <http://www.hse.gov.uk/statistics/causdis/stress/index.htm>

3) BBC Breakfast, 2013. [TV programme], BBC, BBC One, 26 November 2013.

4) Stress Management Society. About stress. [online] Available at: <http://www.stress.org.uk/About-stress.aspx>

5) BBC Lab UK. The Stress Test. [online] Available at: <https://www.bbc.co.uk/labuk/results/stress/index.html>, June 2011

6) Banks, S. (1998). *The missing link: reflections on philosophy and spirit.* Edmonton, Canada: Lone Pine Publishing, p.21.

7) Health and Safety Executive (HSE). What is stress? [online] Available at: <http://www.hse.gov.uk/stress/furtheradvice/whatisstress.htm>

Chapter 5

1) Rosenthal, R. and Jacobson, L. (1968). *Pygmalion in the classroom: Teacher expectation and pupils' intellectual development.* New York: Holt, Rinehart & Winston.

2) *Hypnosurgery Live*, 2006. [TV programme], Zig Zag Productions, More 4, 10 April 2006.

3) Kohli, S.C. and Gibb, A. (2005). Jack Stanley Gibson. *BMJ*, 330(7505): 1452. Available at: <http://www.ncbi.nlm.nih.gov/pmc/articles/PMC558395/>

4) *Derren Brown: Fear and Faith*, 2012. [TV programme], Objective Productions, Channel 4, 9 November 2012.

5) *Horizon: the power of the placebo*, 2014. [TV programme], BBC, BBC Two, 17 February 2014.

6) Langer, E.J. (1979). *Counterclockwise: mindful health and the power of possibility.* London: Hodder & Stoughton.

7) Lipton, B. (2005). *The biology of belief: unleashing the power of consciousness, matter and miracles.* Mountain of Love Productions.

8) Lipton, B. (2011). *Spontaneous evolution: our positive future and a way to get there from here.* Mountain of Love Productions.

8) Cloud, J. (2010). Why your DNA isn't your destiny. TIME [online] Available at: <http://content.time.com/time/magazine/article/0,9171,1952313,00.html>

9) Lipton, B. Living is Easy, radio show podcast [online] Available at: <http://www.livingiseasy.com.au/podcasts/bruce-lipton-1/>

10) Sakai, J. (2013). Study reveals gene expression changes with meditation. University of Wisconsin–Madison [online] Available at:< http://www.news.wisc.edu/22370>

Chapter 6

1) Naish, J. (2009). Is multi-tasking bad for your brain? Experts reveal the hidden perils of juggling too many jobs. [online] Available at: < http://www.dailymail.co.uk/health/article-1205669/Is-multi-tasking-bad-brain-Experts-reveal-hidden-perils-juggling-jobs.html>

2) Mark, G. The cost of interrupted work: more speed and stress [online] Available: <https://www.ics.uci.edu/~gmark/chi08-mark.pdf>

3) *Fawlty Towers: the Germans* (1975). [TV programme], BBC, BBC Two, 24 October 1975.

4) Watts, A. (1954). *The wisdom of insecurity.* New York: Rider & Co.

5) Mark, G., Ibid.

6) Sutherland, R. Perspective is everything. [online] Available at: < www.ted.com/talks/rory_sutherland_perspective_is_everything?language=en>

Chapter 7

1) HM Revenue and Customs (HMRC), (2012). Find 'inner peace' – do

your tax return now. [online] Available at: < https://www.gov.uk/government/news/find-inner-peace-do-your-tax-return-now>

2) Watts, A. (1954). *The wisdom of insecurity.* New York: Rider & Co.

3) Frankl, V.E. (2004). *Man's search for meaning: the classic tribute to hope from the Holocaust.* London: Rider. Translated from German in 1946.

Chapter 8

1) Jeffers, S. (2007). *Feel the fear and do it anyway: how to turn your fear and indecision into confidence and action.* Revised and updated edition. London: Vermilion.

Chapter 9

1) Vonnegut, K. (1982). *Deadeye Dick.* New York: Bantam Doubleday Dell Publishing Group.

2) Maslow, A.H. (1943). A theory of human motivation. *Psychological Review,* 50 (4), 370–96.

Chapter 10

1) Spittle, E. (2010). *Our true identity … three principles.* CreateSpace Independent Publishing Platform.

2) Kausen, R.C. (2003). *We've got to stop meeting like this!* Chicago, IL: Life Education.

3) Barsade, S.G. and O'Neill, O.A. (2014). What's love got to do with it?: the influence of a culture of companionate love in the long-term care setting. *Administrative Science Quarterly,* (forthcoming).

4) HBR Blog Network. Barsade, S.G. and O'Neill, O.A. (2014). Employees who feel love perform better. [online]. Available at: <http://blogs.hbr.org/2014/01/employees-who-feel-love-perform-better/>

5) Bolte Taylor, J. (2008). *My stroke of insight: a brain scientist's personal journey.* London: Hodder & Stoughton.

Chapter 11

1) Mikels, J. A., Maglio, S. J., Reed, A.E. and Kaplowitz, L.J. (2011). Should I go with my gut? Investigating the benefits of emotion-focused decision making. *Emotion*, 11 (4), 743–753.

2) Dean, J. (2011). Feelings beat thoughts for fast complex decisions. [online] Available at: < http://www.spring.org.uk/2011/09/quick-decisions-go-with-your-gut.php>

3) Godin, S. (2012). *The Icarus deception: how high will you fly?* New York: Penguin.

Chapter 12

1) Mills, R. (1996). *Realizing mental health: toward a new psychology of resiliency.* New York: Sulzburger & Graham Publishing.

About the Author

Chantal Burns is a state of mind and performance specialist and has worked with organisations for 27 years.

She has managed and led commercial teams generating multimillion pound revenues in fiercely competitive markets within large corporates and start-ups.

Over the past 14 years, Chantal has taught and consulted internationally with thousands of people at all levels from new starters to CEOs across many sectors.

In 2012 Chantal introduced state of mind *'principles based'* education in Japan, where she has been teaching 'state of mind' programmes for the past three years. Her organisation was also the first to bring this transformative education to Social Care leaders in the UK.

Chantal's passion is showing people and organisations the incredible influence they have over their own mental wellbeing and performance.

The benefits available when we *put state of mind first* are unlimited and include our performance and fulfilment at work, at home and in the wider communities in which we live.

Through a simple understanding of how we function, we all have unlimited potential to live in high levels of mental wellbeing and clarity.

From this level of wellbeing and clarity, we can make powerful and healthy choices and changes and discover new possibilities beyond the limitations of our thinking.

To read her blogs and articles visit www.chantalburns.com and to stay connected, you can follow her on twitter@chantalburns

If you want to get updates on events, free resources or the latest research, sign up to her newsletters at www.chantalburns.com

Acknowledgements

My research and this resulting book have been a labour of love.

When I embarked on the research in 2012, I had no idea where it would lead. I could never have completed this project without the help, love and wisdom of so many wonderful friends, colleagues, mentors, clients and family. It would fill too many pages if I mentioned everyone, so a big thank you to you all. If I have missed anyone, please know that I appreciate and value you.

My special thanks to...

All my clients over the past 16 years. You are my greatest teachers.

All the inspirational leaders that I've interviewed and all those who participated in the research.

Dr Mark Howard for your wisdom, guidance and friendship and for reminding me of what matters.

Linda Ramus, for your help and encouragement.

Dr Bill Pettit, for your feedback, friendship and support.

Cheryl Bond for being a fab friend and wise ear.

Mary Wheater for our inspiring conversations.

Vivienne Edgecombe for kicking off the feedback process.

Keith Blevens PhD and Valda Munroe, for your rigour and for guiding me back to clarity in every conversation.

Mulberrys, my second office. What would I have done without you all!

Sarah Messer for all your invaluable help during the set up of the research.

Claudette Parry for your creative spark and support and for indulging me in my crazy moments.

Jemma Smith at NSM Research for being so patient, kind and thorough in helping me to navigate my way through the vast number of tabulations and research findings.

Robert Kausen, I cherish the time we've spent together exploring the spiritual nature of life.

And to my friends, colleagues and mentors

Garret Kramer, for your friendship and uncompromising honesty.

Jamie Smart for pointing me in this direction and for being a great friend, especially in those moments when I hit the wall.

Shaa Wasmund for your belief that anything is possible.

Dicken, Ami, Annika, Gabriela, Jack, George, Linda, Don, Terri, Aaron, Mara, Cathy, Judy, Robin, Jan, Chip, Elsie and Joe – thank you.

Daren Rubens for the original spark that first ignited this project, for your unswerving honesty and for being a true example of authentic leadership.

The late Sydney Banks for sharing what he saw and for showing us the way.

The very early pioneers of this understanding for their tireless and extraordinary work; the late Dr Roger Mills, Dr George Pransky, Dr Rita J. Schuford, Keith Blevens PhD.

To Monique, for being you, for always being there and for your constant support and encouragement.

Dr Christina Hall, I could never thank you enough for all your friendship, love and mentoring over the past 10 years.

Andy, you are my rock. Thank you for your patience, the endless supply of tea and too many dinners for me to ever make up for!

And to the wonderful team at Pearson for helping me to get this out into the world.

Publisher's acknowledgements

We are grateful to the following for permission to reproduce copyright material:

Photo

Photo on p.113 HM Revenue & Customs, SA Campaign press ad – builder (http://www.mynewsdesk.com/uk/hm-revenue-customs-hmrc/images/sa-campaign-press-ad-builder-169875), Creative Commons Attribution 3.0, http://creativecommons.org/licenses/by/3.0/)

In some instances we have been unable to trace the owners of copyright material, and we would appreciate any information that would enable us to do so.

ThoughtWorks is our suite of programmes that bring a Principles based understanding of state of mind to all organisa-  tional and performance areas from leadership and change to personal effectiveness, influence and sales.

Most training, coaching and people development programmes are grounded in *information or content* based learning which tend to be skill and strategy based.

The success of these types of programmes is dependent on successful implementation and application of knowledge and skills. And the successful application and practical use of information, new processes, techniques or strategies is based on the grounding or the performance platform of the individual – i.e. their understanding of what really drives their performance.

An understanding of the operating principles behind our performance is what gives organisations and individuals the strongest and healthiest platform to work and live from. This operating platform is responsible for all the attributes of a high-performance mindset. It brings mental clarity and perspective in moments of challenge when the mind most needs it. It connects people to their natural creativity and motivation. It gives change efforts the best chances of succeeding. It fosters great relationships, winning teams and dynamic and resilient organisations.

If you want to explore how you can create a more powerful performance platform for yourself or your organisation, you can reach the author as follows;

Email: **Chantal@starconsultancy.com**
Telephone: **+44 (0)7958 224175**
Twitter: **@Chantalburns**
Websites: **For free resources visit: www.chantalburns.com; www. starconsultancy.com**

If you are a leader, manager or you have responsibility for the performance, motivation and engagement of others, then you may be interested in **The Missing KPI**,  a leader's guide exploring the strategic and organisational implications of state of mind in the workplace and includes key research insights. Find out more by contacting the author at chantal@starconsultancy.com.

Index

Page numbers in **bold** refer to glossary definitions